American History

Interactive Notebook: The Civil War

Grades 5–8

Author: Schyrlet Cameron

Editor: Mary Dieterich

Proofreaders: Alexis Fey and Margaret Brown

COPYRIGHT © 2022 Mark Twain Media, Inc.

ISBN 978-1-62223-860-6

Printing No. CD-405068

Mark Twain Media, Inc., Publishers
Distributed by Carson Dellosa Education

Table of Contents

Introduction

Interactive Notebook: The Civil War is one of several books in Mark Twain Media's new American History Series of interactive notebooks. This series provides students in grades 5 through 8 with opportunities to explore the significant events and people that make up American history.

Creating and Using an Interactive Notebook

Interactive Notebook: The Civil War is designed to allow students to become active participants in their own learning. The book lays out an easy-to-follow plan for setting up, creating, and maintaining the interactive notebook. Once completed, the notebook becomes a great resource for reviewing and studying for tests.

How the Book Is Organized

The 19 lessons contained in Interactive Notebook: The Civil War cover five units of study: Road to War, Secession, First Part of the Civil War, Second Part of the Civil War, and Victory for the North. The units can be used in the order presented or in an order that best fits the classroom or home school curriculum. Teachers can easily differentiate units to address the individual learning levels and needs of students. The lessons are designed to support state and national standards. Each lesson consists of three pages. Teachers need to make the necessary number of copies of the Student Instructions, Key Details, and Left-hand Pages for each student to use. Students then use those pages to create the left- and right-hand pages of their interactive notebooks.

- **Right-hand page:** essential information for understanding the lesson concepts. Answers to the Demonstrate and Reflect activities can be written on this page, or an additional page may need to be added for those answers.
- **Left-hand page:** hands-on activity such as a foldable or graphic organizer to help students process essential information from the lesson.

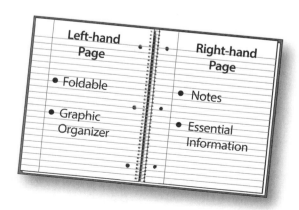

Organizing an Interactive Notebook

What Is an Interactive Notebook?

Does this sound familiar? "I can't find my homework…class notes…study guide." If so, the interactive notebook is a tool students can use to help manage this problem. An interactive notebook is simply a notebook that students use to record, store, and organize their work. The "interactive" aspect of the notebook comes from the fact that students are working with information in various ways as they fill in the notebook. Once completed, the notebook becomes the student's own personalized study guide and a great resource for reviewing information, reinforcing concepts, and studying for tests.

Materials Needed to Create an Interactive Notebook

- Notebook (spiral, composition, or binder with loose-leaf paper)
- Glue stick
- Scissors
- Colored pencils (we do not recommend using markers)
- Tabs

Creating an Interactive Notebook

A good time to introduce the interactive notebook is at the beginning of a new unit of study. Use the following steps to get started.

Step 1: *Notebook Cover*
Students design a cover to reflect the units of study. They should add their name and other important information as directed by the teacher.

Step 2: *Grading Rubric*
Take time to discuss the grading rubric with the students. It is important for each student to understand the expectations for creating the interactive notebook.

Step 3: *Table of Contents*
Students label the first several pages of the notebook "Table of Contents." When completing a new page, they then add its title to the table of contents.

Step 4: *Creating Pages*
The notebook is developed using the dual-page format. The right-hand side is the input page where essential information, Demonstrate and Reflect answers, and notes from readings, lectures, or videos are placed. The left-hand side is the output page reserved for folding activities, charts, graphic organizers, etc. Students number the front and back of each page in the bottom outside corner (odd: LEFT-side; even: RIGHT-side).

Step 5: *Tab Units*
Add a tab to the edge of the first page of each unit to make it easy to flip to the unit.

Step 6: *Glossary*
Students reserve several pages at the back of the notebook where they can create a glossary of domain-specific terms encountered in each lesson.

Step 7: *Pocket*
Students should attach a pocket to the inside of the back cover of the notebook for storage of handouts, returned quizzes, class syllabus, and other items that don't seem to belong on pages of the notebook. This can be an envelope, resealable plastic bag, or students can design their own pocket.

Left-hand and Right-hand Notebook Pages

Interactive notebooks are usually viewed open like a textbook. This allows the student to view the left-hand page and right-hand page at the same time. You have several options for how to format the two pages. Traditionally, the right-hand page is used as the input or the content part of the lesson. The left-hand page is the student output part of the lesson. This is where the students have an opportunity to show what they have learned in a creative and colorful way. (Color helps the brain remember information.) The notebook image on the right details different types of items and activities that could be included for each page.

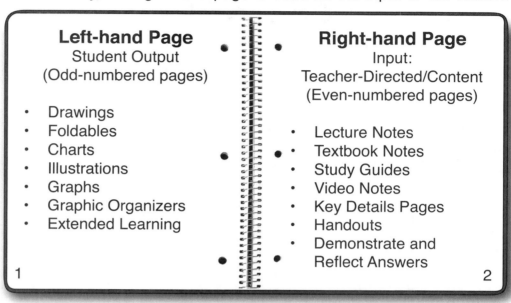

The format of the interactive notebook involves both the right-brain and left-brain hemispheres to help students process information. When creating the pages, start with the left-hand page. First, have students date the page. Students then move to the right-hand page and the teacher-directed part of the lesson. Finally, students use the information they have learned to complete the left-hand page. Below is an example of completed right- and left-hand pages.

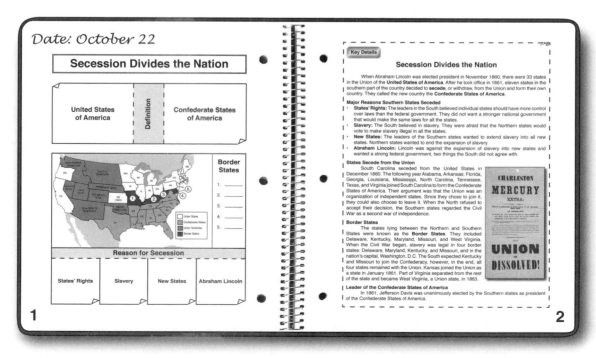

Interactive Notebook Grading Rubric

Directions: Review the criteria for the grading rubric that will be used to score your completed notebook. Place this page in your notebook.

The Civil War Interactive Notebook Grading Rubric

Category	Excellent (4)	Good Work (3)	Needs Improvement (2)	Incomplete (1)
Table of Contents	Table of contents is complete.	Table of contents is mostly complete.	Table of contents is somewhat incomplete.	Attempt was made to include table of contents.
Organization	All notebook pages are in correct order. All are numbered, dated, and titled correctly.	Most pages are in correct order. Most are numbered, dated, and titled correctly.	Some pages are in correct order. Some are numbered, dated, and titled correctly.	Few pages are in correct order. Few are numbered, dated, and titled correctly.
Content	All information complete, accurate, and placed in the correct order. All spelling correct.	Most information complete, accurate, and placed in the correct order. Most spelling correct.	Some information complete, accurate, and placed in the correct order. Some spelling errors.	Few pages correctly completed. Many spelling errors.
Appearance	All notebook pages are neat and colorful.	Most notebook pages are neat and colorful.	Some notebook pages are neat and colorful.	Few notebook pages are neat and colorful.

Teacher's Comments:

Civil War Timeline

1860	Nov. 6	Abraham Lincoln elected president
	Dec. 20	Secession of South Carolina from the Union
1861	Jan.–Feb.	Secession of Mississippi, Florida, Alabama, Georgia, Louisiana, and Texas
	Feb. 9	Confederate government organized; Jefferson Davis selected president
	Mar. 4	Lincoln inaugurated President of the United States
	Apr. 14	Fall of Fort Sumter
	Apr.–Jun.	Secession of Virginia, Arkansas, North Carolina, and Tennessee
	May 20	Richmond, Virginia, named Confederate capital
	Jul. 21	First Battle of Bull Run
	Nov. 6	Confederate states presidential election confirms Jefferson Davis as president for a six-year term
1862	Mar. 9	Navel battle between the *Monitor* and the *Merrimac*
	Apr. 6–7	Battle of Shiloh
	Jun. 1	Robert E. Lee appointed commander of the Army of Northern Virginia
	Aug. 29–30	Second Battle of Bull Run
	Sept. 17	Battle of Antietam
	Dec. 13	Battle of Fredericksburg
1863	Jan. 1	Lincoln issues Emancipation Proclamation
	May 2–4	Battle of Chancellorsville
	May 19–Jul. 4	Siege of Vicksburg
	Jul. 1–3	Battle of Gettysburg
	Sept. 18–20	Battle of Chickamauga
	Nov. 19	Lincoln's address at Gettysburg
	Nov. 23–25	Battle of Chattanooga
1864	Mar. 10	General Grant appointed commander of the Union Army
	May 5–6	Battle of the Wilderness
	May 8–19	Battle of Spotsylvania
	Sept. 2	Sherman captures Atlanta
	Nov. 8	President Lincoln reelected
	Nov. 15	Sherman begins his march to the sea
1865	Apr. 2	Siege of Petersburg ends
	Apr. 3	Union Army captures Richmond, Virginia, capital of the Confederacy
	Apr. 9	Surrender of General Lee and Confederate Army at Appomattox Court House, Virginia, effectively ends the Civil War
	Apr. 15	Assassination of President Lincoln; Andrew Johnson now president

Student Instructions: Events Leading Up to War

Materials Needed

Glue, scissors, colored pencils

How to Create a Right-hand Interactive Notebook Page

Read the Key Details page. Then cut out the page and attach it to the right-hand page of your interactive notebook. Use what you have learned to create the left-hand page.

How to Create a Left-hand Interactive Notebook Page

Complete the following steps to create the left-hand page of your interactive notebook. Use lots of color.

Step 1: Cut out the title and glue it to the top of the notebook page.

Step 2: Cut out the *Constitutional Compromises* flap piece. Cut on the solid line to create two flaps. Apply glue to the back of the gray tab and attach it below the title. Under each flap, explain the compromise.

Step 3: Cut out the *Major Events* flap piece. Cut on the solid lines to create six flaps. Apply glue to the back of the gray center section and attach it at the bottom of the page. Under each flap, explain the event.

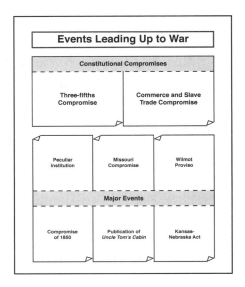

Demonstrate and Reflect on What You Have Learned

The Kansas-Nebraska Act caused a border war on the Kansas-Missouri border. Use the Internet or other reference sources to research the event. What was at the core of the conflict? The struggle was often very violent, earning it several nicknames. What was one of the names? Write the answers in your interactive notebook.

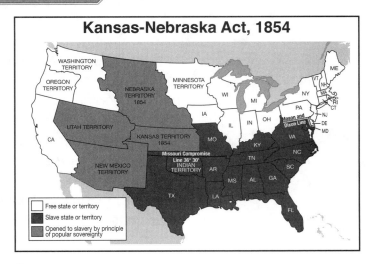

Kansas-Nebraska Act, 1854

Key Details

Events Leading Up to War

The delegates to the **Constitutional Convention** had to **compromise** (come to an agreement) on several key points in order to create a constitution that was agreeable to all states. Several of the compromises dealt with the issue of slavery. The **Three-fifths Compromise** was an agreement that enslaved persons would count as three-fifths of a free man when counting population to determine the number of seats (representatives) the state was allowed in the House of Representatives. The **Commerce and Slave Trade Compromise** gave Congress the right to regulate trade but would not interfere with the slave trade for 20 years.

Events Leading Up to War

- From 1619 to 1856, the **Peculiar Institution** was the term white Southerners used for slavery. The first African-born "servants" arrived from the West Indies in 1619 and were listed as indentured servants. After their time of servitude ended, it is believed that they were freed. By 1675, African servants had become servants for life and then simply "slaves." By the 1700s, slavery was a common practice in all the thirteen colonies.

- **Missouri Compromise of 1820** was passed in Congress to preserve the balance of power in Congress between slave and free states. The Compromise was passed in 1820, admitting Missouri as a slave state and Maine as a free state.

- The issue of slavery became more of a problem at the beginning of the **Mexican-American War**. In 1846, David Wilmot proposed the **Wilmot Proviso** (plan) to Congress to ban slavery in territory acquired from Mexico. The proviso failed after Southerners warned it might lead to **secession**, or withdrawing, from the United States.

- The **Compromise of 1850** was a group of laws passed by Congress to resolve disputes over slavery in new territories added to the United States. The compromise admitted California as a **"free,"** or no slavery, state but allowed some newly acquired territories to decide on slavery for themselves. Part of the Compromise included the **Fugitive Slave Act**, which required runaway slaves to be returned to their owners, even if they were in a free state.

Some of the legislators involved in the Compromise of 1850

- Harriet Beecher Stowe's novel, ***Uncle Tom's Cabin***, was published in 1852. The anti-slavery book changed many people's attitudes toward slavery and enslaved people in the United States. Years later, when President Lincoln was introduced to Mrs. Stowe, Lincoln greeted her with, "So you're the little woman who wrote the book that made this great war!"

- In 1854, Senator Stephen Douglas proposed the **Kansas-Nebraska Act** to Congress. The law created two new territories, each with the option to allow slavery if the people chose. Many Northerners protested this violation of the Missouri Compromise, which barred slavery from that region.

Events Leading Up to War

Constitutional Compromises

Three-fifths Compromise	Commerce and Slave Trade Compromise

Peculiar Institution	Missouri Compromise	Wilmot Proviso

Major Events

Compromise of 1850	Publication of *Uncle Tom's Cabin*	Kansas-Nebraska Act

Student Instructions: The Abolitionist Movement

Materials Needed

Glue, scissors, colored pencils

How to Create a Right-hand Interactive Notebook Page

Read the Key Details page. Then cut out the box and attach it to the right-hand page of your interactive notebook. Use what you have learned to create the left-hand page.

How to Create a Left-hand Interactive Notebook Page

Complete the following steps to create the left-hand page of your interactive notebook. Use lots of color.

Step 1: Cut out the title and glue it to the top of the notebook page.

Step 2: Cut out the *Abolitionist* flap book. Cut on the solid lines to create six flaps. Apply glue to the back of the gray center section and attach it below the title. Complete the sentence on the gray section.

Step 3: Under each flap, explain the person's contribution to the abolitionist movement.

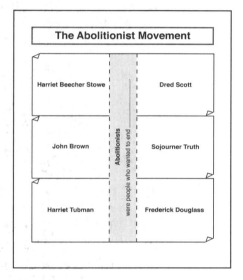

Demonstrate and Reflect on What You Have Learned

Nat Turner was an enslaved Black man and also a Christian preacher. Use the Internet or other reference sources to research the outcome of the four-day-long conflict known as Nat Turner's Rebellion in 1831. Why did Nat Turner rebel, and what was the result of the conflict? Write the answers in your interactive notebook. Support your answers with specific details or examples.

Artist's drawing of Nat Turner, who led a band of enslaved people against white slave owners in 1831.

Key Details

The Abolitionist Movement

Thomas Jefferson (a slave owner from Virginia) included ideas from members of the Continental Congress, as well as his own ideas about freedom, to write the Declaration of Independence. In the first draft, he included a provision that abolished slavery. That section was deleted by the Continental Congress before it was signed in 1776.

Abolitionists were people who wanted to end slavery. **The Society of Friends**, or Quakers, of Pennsylvania were the earliest group in America to protest slavery. In 1688, four members of the Society of Friends published the first antislavery resolution in America.

Harriet Beecher Stowe wrote the book *Uncle Tom's Cabin* about the difficult lives of enslaved people. The book was banned in the South, but it sold over 500,000 copies in the first five years. Harriet's book helped readers see slaves as real people in an unjust and cruel situation.

Despite the Fugitive Slave Law, many enslaved people still tried to escape. A group of people helped them by running the **Underground Railroad**, a series of secret paths and trails that led to free states and Canada. Along the route to freedom, runaways stayed in **safe houses** and hiding places called **stations** where they could eat and rest before continuing their journey. Men and women, both Black and white, became **conductors**, or guides, and **station masters**, or people who hid runaways in their homes, on the Underground Railroad.

John Brown recruited supporters and established a refuge for fugitive slaves in the mountains of Virginia. On October 16, 1859, with a force of 18 men, including three of his sons, he seized the United States arsenal at **Harpers Ferry, Virginia**, and won control of the town. Brown was wounded and forced to surrender. He was arrested and charged with various crimes, including treason and murder. After being found guilty, John Brown was hanged in Charlestown, Virginia, in December 1859.

Harriet Tubman was born into slavery on a Maryland plantation around 1820. When Harriet learned that her owner planned to sell her, she ran away. She took the Underground Railroad to Pennsylvania where slavery was illegal. After she was free, Harriet made 19 trips into slave-holding states and led over 300 enslaved people to freedom.

Harriet Tubman

Dred Scott v. Sanford was a United States Supreme Court decision. Dred Scott was a Black enslaved man. He filed suit in Missouri state court in 1846 for his freedom and lost. He argued that the time he had spent in a free state and a free territory had made him free. In 1857, the Supreme court ruled that Black people, whether free or slaves, were not citizens of the United States so they could not sue in federal court.

Sojourner Truth was born into slavery in New York about 1797. After she escaped slavery in 1827, she became the first Black woman to successfully sue a white man in order to have one of her children returned to her. She became a preacher and went on speaking tours for the abolitionist cause. She also unsuccessfully petitioned the government to grant former slaves land in the West where they could settle.

Frederick Douglass was a man who had escaped slavery in Maryland. He became one of the most famous Black activists, authors, and public speakers. He was a leader in the abolitionist movement and published the abolitionist newspaper *The North Star*.

The Abolitionist Movement

Harriet Beecher Stowe	Dred Scott
John Brown	Sojourner Truth
Harriet Tubman	Frederick Douglass

Abolitionists were people who wanted to end _____

Student Instructions: Presidential Election of 1860

Materials Needed

Glue, scissors, colored pencils

How to Create a Right-hand Interactive Notebook Page

Read the Key Details page. Then cut out the box and attach it to the right-hand page of your interactive notebook. Use what you have learned to create the left-hand page.

How to Create a Left-hand Interactive Notebook Page

Complete the following steps to create the left-hand page of your interactive notebook. Use lots of color.

Step 1: Cut out the title and glue it to the top of the notebook page.

Step 2: Complete the *Political Party* piece. Write the definition and use the term in a sentence. Apply glue to the back of the piece and attach it below the title.

Step 3: Complete the *1860 Presidential Candidates* chart. Cut out the chart. Apply glue to the back and attach it at the bottom of the page.

Presidential Election of 1860

Political Party	Definition	
	Sentence	

1860 Presidential Candidates

Candidates	Political Party	Views on Slavery
Abraham Lincoln		
Stephen Douglas		
John C. Breckenridge		
John Bell		

Demonstrate and Reflect on What You Have Learned

Use the Internet or other reference sources to research the presidential election of 1860. Color the map to show the states won by each candidate. Complete the Map Legend. Cut out the map and glue it in your interactive notebook

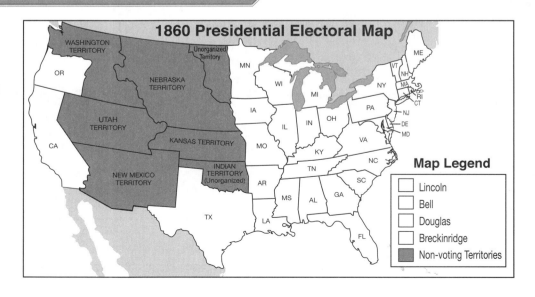

1860 Presidential Electoral Map

Map Legend
- Lincoln
- Bell
- Douglas
- Breckinridge
- Non-voting Territories

Key Details

Presidential Election of 1860

The 1860 presidential election focused on several issues, including slavery.

1860 Political Parties and Candidates

A **political party** is a group of people that is organized based on its beliefs and goals on how to govern a country. In the 1860 presidential election, several political parties nominated rival candidates for president.

The **Republican Party** was **founded** (established) in 1854. The newly formed political party nominated **Abraham Lincoln** as its presidential candidate. Lincoln stated his views on slavery very clearly during his campaign. "I will not abolish slavery where it already exists, but we must not let the practice spread. I am opposed to allowing slavery in the new territories." In the 1800s, many candidates had nicknames. Abe Lincoln was known as "the Railsplitter" and "Honest Abe."

The **Democratic Party** was founded in 1828. **Stephen Douglas** was nominated as the Democratic presidential candidate. Stephen Douglas was nicknamed the "Little Giant." Douglas wanted the people in new states to decide the issue of slavery for themselves.

Conflict arose between the radical and conservative Democrats. A separate convention of radical **Southern Democrats** nominated their own candidate, **John C. Breckenridge** of Kentucky. Breckinridge strongly supported slavery.

The **Constitutional Unionist** party formed in 1859. Members wanted to avoid **secession**, withdrawal from the Union of the United States. They did not take a firm stand either for or against slavery or its expansion. They nominated **John Bell** of Tennessee.

Election Results

The president of the United States is not determined by the **popular vote**, or the number of citizens voting for the candidate. Instead, when people vote for president, they are really voting for an **elector**, a person from their state. Each state has a certain number of electors. These electors then vote for president. To become president, one candidate needed at least 152 electoral votes. When the electoral votes were counted, Lincoln had clearly won.

Candidate	Popular Votes	Electoral Votes
Abraham Lincoln	1,766,452	180
Stephen Douglas	1,376,957	12
John C. Breckenridge	849,781	72
John Bell	588,879	39

Lincoln won in all states in the North as well as in California and Oregon. Breckenridge won all states in the South, plus Maryland and Delaware. Bell won in Tennessee, Kentucky, and Virginia. Although Douglas had the second most popular votes, he only won in Missouri and part of New Jersey, giving him the lowest number of electoral votes.

Presidential Election of 1860

Political Party	Definition
	Sentence

1860 Presidential Candidates		
Candidates	**Political Party**	**Views on Slavery**
Abraham Lincoln		
Stephen Douglas		
John C. Breckenridge		
John Bell		

Student Instructions: Causes of the Civil War

Materials Needed

Glue, scissors, colored pencils

How to Create a Right-hand Interactive Notebook Page

Read the Key Details page. Then cut out the page and attach it to the right-hand page of your interactive notebook. Use what you have learned to create the left-hand page.

How to Create a Left-hand Interactive Notebook Page

Complete the following steps to create the left-hand page of your interactive notebook. Use lots of color.

Step 1: Cut out the title and glue it to the top of the notebook page.

Step 2: Cut out the *What Does it Mean?* flap book. Apply glue to the back of the gray center section and attach it below the title. Under each flap, explain the term.

Step 3: Cut out the *United States in 1860* flap book. Cut on the solid lines to create five flaps. Apply glue to the back of the map section and attach it at the bottom of the page. Under each flap, explain the disagreement between the North and the South.

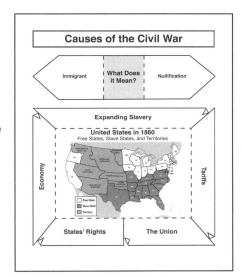

Demonstrate and Reflect on What You Have Learned

Eli Whitney invented the cotton gin in 1793. Use the Internet or other reference sources to research the invention. What affect did the cotton gin have on the economy of the South? Write the answer in your interactive notebook. Support your answer with specific details or examples.

Enslaved people using the first cotton gin

Key Details

Causes of the Civil War

The states of the nation were held together by a fragile cord by the 1860s. Besides the disagreement between the North and South about the **legality** (lawfulness) and **morality** (decency) of slavery, there were other differences.

Economy

The **economy**, or the financial system, of the South was based on agriculture and the production of cotton. Large farms were called **plantations**. Enslaved people from Africa were used as the labor force. **Slaves** were considered property and were forced to work without pay or personal rights.

The North had many factories like the Southwark Foundry in Philadelphia, PA.

The economy of the North was based on manufacturing and trade. The South depended on the North for manufactured goods. The factories used low-paid immigrants from Europe and Asia to do the hardest jobs. An **immigrant** is a person who moves from one place to another to find work or better living conditions.

Expansion of Slavery

Not only did the North and South disagree about the lawfulness and morality of slavery, but they also disagreed about extending slavery into the West. Northerners wanted to end the expansion of slavery. Slave owners wanted to extend slavery to all new states.

Tariffs

Southern farmers and plantation owners wanted to sell their cotton to other countries and buy manufactured goods as cheaply as possible because the South had few factories. They did not want to pay **tariffs** (taxes on goods brought in from another country).

Northern factory owners wanted high tariffs on imported goods so they could sell their own products in the United States. They wanted to keep out the competition by making foreign goods more expensive.

States' Rights

Northerners felt the federal government should have more power than any individual state. Southerners believed individual states should have more control over laws than the federal government. This resulted in the idea of **nullification**, where the states would have the right to rule federal laws unconstitutional. The federal government denied states this right.

The Union

Northerners believed the United States must remain one country to stay strong. Southerners claimed that the United States was an organization of independent states. Since they chose to join the Union, they could also choose to leave it and form their own country.

Causes of the Civil War

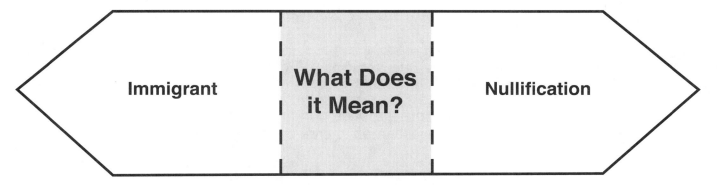

Immigrant

What Does it Mean?

Nullification

Expanding Slavery

Economy

Tariffs

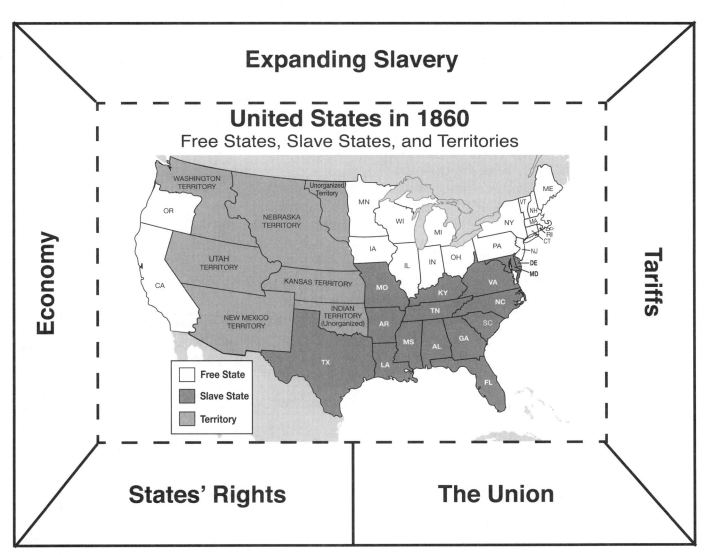

United States in 1860
Free States, Slave States, and Territories

☐ Free State
■ Slave State
▨ Territory

States' Rights

The Union

Student Instructions: Secession Divides the Nation

Materials Needed

Glue, scissors, colored pencils

How to Create a Right-hand Interactive Notebook Page

Read the Key Details page. Then cut out the page and attach it to the right-hand page of your interactive notebook. Use what you have learned to create the left-hand page.

How to Create a Left-hand Interactive Notebook Page

Complete the following steps to create the left-hand page of your interactive notebook. Use lots of color.

Step 1: Cut out the title and glue it to the top of the notebook page.

Step 2: Cut out the *Definition* flap book. Apply glue to the gray center section and attach it below the title. Under each flap, write the definition.

Step 3: Complete the *Border States* section of the *Reason for Secession* flap book. Fill in the numbered blanks with the abbreviation of the corresponding numbered Border State on the map. If you need help, use the Internet or an atlas.

Step 4: Cut out the *Reason for Secession* flap book. Apply glue to the back of the map section and attach it at the bottom of the page. Under each flap, explain the reason for secession.

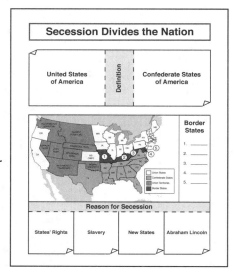

Demonstrate and Reflect on What You Have Learned

The Fugitive Slave Acts were federal laws that allowed for the capture and return of runaway slaves within the territory of the United States. Use the Internet or other reference sources to research the Acts. How did the laws increase the tensions between the North and the South? How did they contribute to the eventual secession of the South and the Civil War? Write the answers in your interactive notebook. Support your answers with specific details or examples.

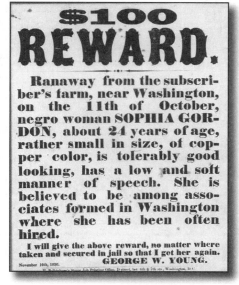

An 1858 reward broadside (poster) for a runaway slave.

Key Details

Secession Divides the Nation

When Abraham Lincoln was elected president in November 1860, there were 33 states in the Union of the **United States of America**. Between the date of the election and shortly after he took office in 1861, eleven states in the southern part of the country decided to **secede**, or withdraw, from the Union and form their own country. They called the new country the **Confederate States of America**.

Major Reasons Southern States Seceded
- **States' Rights:** The leaders in the South believed individual states should have more control over laws than the federal government. They did not want a stronger national government that would make the same laws for all the states.
- **Slavery:** The South believed in slavery. They were afraid that the Northern states would vote to make slavery illegal in all the states.
- **New States:** The leaders of the Southern states wanted to extend slavery into all new states. Northern states wanted to end the expansion of slavery.
- **Abraham Lincoln:** Lincoln was against the expansion of slavery into new states and wanted a strong federal government, two things the South did not agree with.

States Secede from the Union
South Carolina seceded from the United States in December 1860. The following year Alabama, Arkansas, Florida, Georgia, Louisiana, Mississippi, North Carolina, Tennessee, Texas, and Virginia joined South Carolina to form the Confederate States of America. Their argument was that the Union was an organization of independent states. Since they chose to join it, they could also choose to leave it. When the North refused to accept their decision, the Southern states regarded the Civil War as a second war of independence.

Border States
The states lying between the Northern and Southern states were known as the **Border States**. They included Delaware, Kentucky, Maryland, Missouri, and West Virginia. When the Civil War began, slavery was legal in four border states: Delaware, Maryland, Kentucky, and Missouri, and in the nation's capital, Washington, D.C. The South expected Kentucky and Missouri to join the Confederacy, however, in the end, all four states remained with the Union. Kansas joined the Union as a state in January 1861. Part of Virginia separated from the rest of the state and became West Virginia, a Union state, in 1863.

CHARLESTON MERCURY EXTRA:

Passed unanimously at 1.15 o'clock, P. M. December 20th, 1860.

AN ORDINANCE

To dissolve the Union between the State of South Carolina and other States united with her under the compact entitled "The Constitution of the United States of America."

We, the People of the State of South Carolina, in Convention assembled, do declare and ordain, and it is hereby declared and ordained,

That the Ordinance adopted by us in Convention, on the twenty-third day of May, in the year of our Lord one thousand seven hundred and eighty-eight, whereby the Constitution of the United States of America was ratified, and also, all Acts and parts of Acts of the General Assembly of this State, ratifying amendments of the said Constitution, are hereby repealed; and that the union now subsisting between South Carolina and other States, under the name of "The United States of America," is hereby dissolved.

THE UNION IS DISSOLVED!

Leader of the Confederate States of America
In 1861, Jefferson Davis was unanimously elected by the Southern states as president of the Confederate States of America.

Secession Divides the Nation

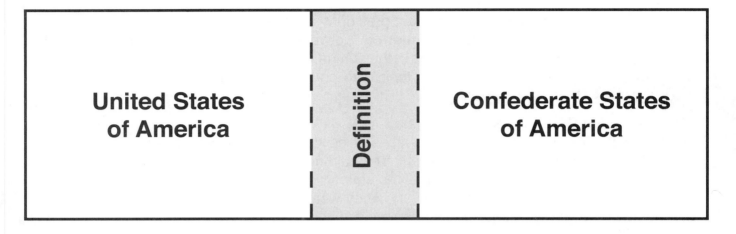

United States of America	Definition	Confederate States of America

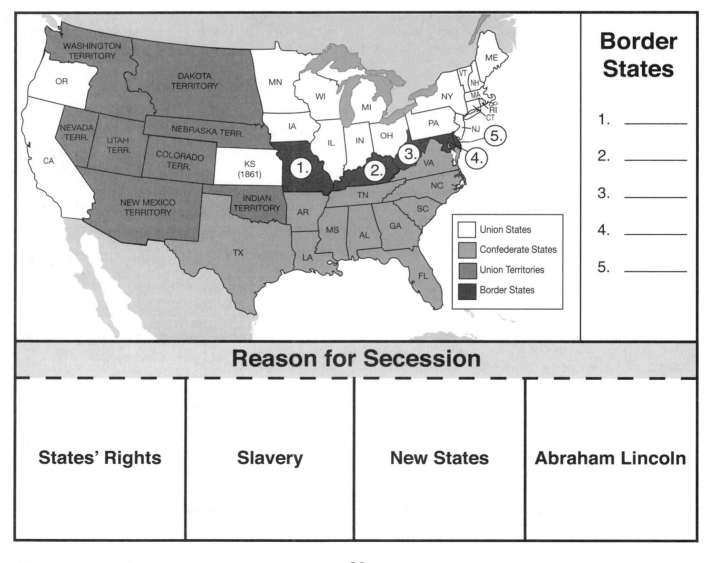

Border States

1. _____
2. _____
3. _____
4. _____
5. _____

Union States
Confederate States
Union Territories
Border States

Reason for Secession

States' Rights	Slavery	New States	Abraham Lincoln

Student Instructions: Abraham Lincoln vs. Jefferson Davis

Materials Needed

Glue, scissors, colored pencils

How to Create a Right-hand Interactive Notebook Page

Read the Key Details page. Then cut out the section and attach it to the right-hand page of your interactive notebook. Use what you have learned to create the left-hand page.

How to Create a Left-hand Interactive Notebook Page

Complete the following steps to create the left-hand page of your interactive notebook. Use lots of color.

Step 1: Cut out the title and glue it to the top of the notebook page.

Step 2: Cut out the *Definition* flap book. Cut on the solid lines to create two flaps. Apply glue to the back of the gray tab and attach it below the title. Under each flap, write the definition.

Step 3: Cut out the *How Were They Different?* flap book. Apply glue to the back of the gray center section and attach it at the bottom of the page. Under each flap, describe the person's education, military experience, pollical life, and attitude toward the presidency.

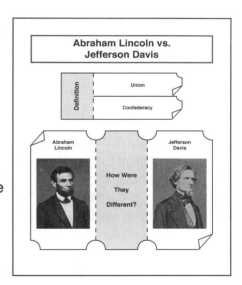

Demonstrate and Reflect on What You Have Learned

Think about what you learned from the reading selection. In some ways, Abraham Lincoln and Jefferson Davis faced similar situations as president. In your interactive notebook, explain how their situations were similar. Support your answer with specific details or examples.

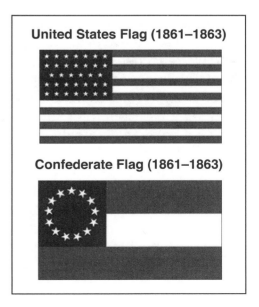

Abraham Lincoln vs. Jefferson Davis

In 1860, just before the Civil War, there were a total of 33 states in the Union. "Union" refers to the union of the United States of America. Eleven Southern states **seceded**, or withdrew, from the Union from 1860 to 1861. The states that seceded from the Union formed a new nation, the Confederate States of America (CSA). It was also called the **Confederacy**.

Jefferson Davis: President of the Confederate States of America

Jefferson Davis was disappointed when he was chosen president of the Confederate States of America. Unlike Lincoln, who had worked hard to become president of the United States, Davis did not want the job; he would have much preferred being a general. Davis had an impressive record. Educated at Transylvania University and West Point, he had been an army officer in the Northwest and was wounded in battle during the Mexican-American War. He was elected to both the House and Senate. In 1853, Davis became Secretary of War. He returned to the Senate in 1857, where he remained until 1861. He opposed secession, but after the decision was made, he supported it. Davis was selected as president of the Confederate States of America in February 1861. He was later elected as president in a general election of the Southern states in November 1861.

Abraham Lincoln: President of the United States of America

Abraham Lincoln was born in Kentucky, and his family migrated to Illinois. He never attended college, but he read enough to qualify as a lawyer. His military service was a brief stint as a militia captain during the Black Hawk War in 1832. He served four terms in the Illinois state legislature and one term in the U.S. House of Representatives. Perhaps the greatest compliment paid to Lincoln during his lifetime was by the Southern newspaper, the Charleston *Mercury*, which said that he ran the presidency with "a bold, steady hand, a vigilant, active eye, a sleepless energy, a fanatic spirit ... and a singleness of purpose that might almost be called patriotic."

Comparing Lincoln and Davis

In some ways, the two men faced similar situations. Both came under fire from the press and were accused of acting like dictators. Each had a Congress that seemed more concerned about getting friends into high places and offering unhelpful suggestions than winning the war. Each wasted valuable time at long cabinet meetings instead of letting the heads of departments do their jobs. Both men carried the burden of long casualty lists and many citizens accusing them of not doing everything possible to end the conflict.

The main difference between the two was that Lincoln was far superior as a politician. Often exhausted and tense, he listened carefully to those who lined up outside his office "for a brief word." He visited military hospitals, shaking hands with the troops, knowing that their relatives voted. Lincoln often delayed making decisions until public opinion was strongly behind the policy he intended to pursue in the first place. Davis did not play the political game, stubbornly pushing unpopular policies.

Abraham Lincoln vs. Jefferson Davis

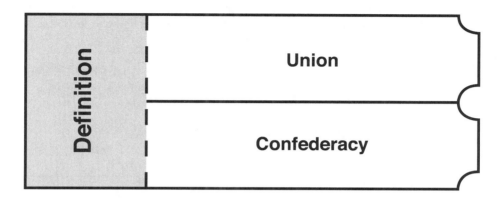

Definition

Union

Confederacy

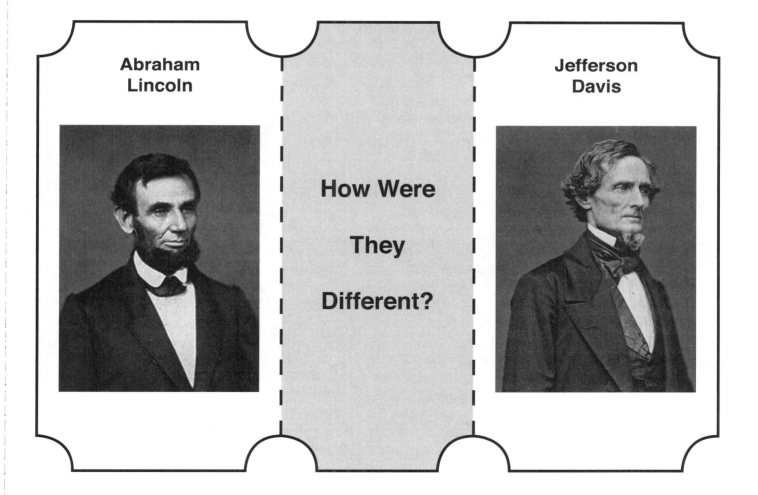

Abraham Lincoln

How Were They Different?

Jefferson Davis

Student Instructions: Attack on Fort Sumter

Materials Needed

Glue, scissors, colored pencils

How to Create a Right-hand Interactive Notebook Page

Read the Key Details page. Then cut out the page and attach it to the right-hand page of your interactive notebook. Use what you have learned to create the left-hand page.

How to Create a Left-hand Interactive Notebook Page

Complete the following steps to create the left-hand page of your interactive notebook. Use lots of color.

Step 1: Cut out the title and glue it to the top of the notebook page.

Step 2: Fill in the result of each event on the four puzzle pieces. Cut out the puzzle pieces. Apply glue to the back of each piece and attach them below the title.

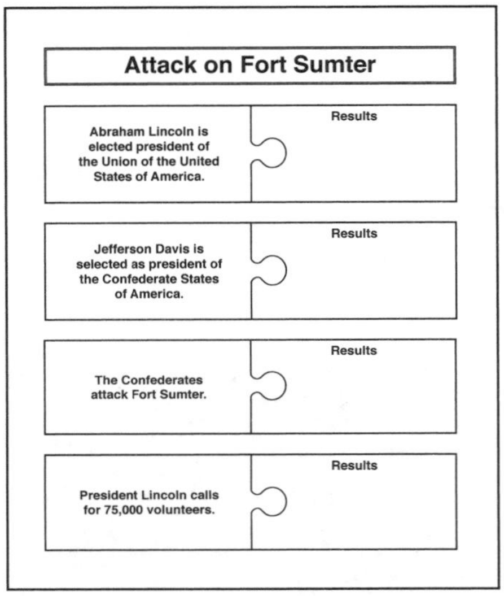

Attack on Fort Sumter
Abraham Lincoln is elected president of the Union of the United States of America. — Results
Jefferson Davis is selected as president of the Confederate States of America. — Results
The Confederates attack Fort Sumter. — Results
President Lincoln calls for 75,000 volunteers. — Results

Demonstrate and Reflect on What You Have Learned

On April 16, 1861, President Lincoln called for 75,000 volunteers to serve in the militia following the bombardment and surrender of Fort Sumter. Soon after, four more Southern states left the Union: Virginia, Arkansas, North Carolina, and Tennessee. Use the Internet to research the date each state seceded from the Union. Use the information to complete the chart to the right. Cut out the chart and glue it in your interactive notebook.

State	Date Seceded from the Union
Virginia	
Arkansas	
North Carolina	
Tennessee	

Key Details

Attack on Fort Sumter

Abraham Lincoln was elected president of the **Union of the United States of America** in November of 1860. As a result of the election, South Carolina **seceded**, or withdrew, from the Union. Mississippi, Alabama, Georgia, Florida, Louisiana, and Texas joined South Carolina, forming the **Confederate States of America**.

In February 1861, Jefferson Davis was selected as president of the Confederate States. He immediately ordered all federal troops of the United States to leave all government forts and buildings in Confederate territory. Abraham Lincoln refused to comply with the order and pledged to maintain control of all federal property.

Confederates Test Lincoln

Soon after Lincoln's **inauguration**, or ceremony of being sworn into office as president, the Confederates tested his vow to hold federal property. Fort Sumter was off the coast of South Carolina and was the property of the United States government. South Carolina, now a Confederate state, demanded Major Robert Anderson surrender the fort.

The North and South both watched to see what Lincoln would do as president. As in his inaugural address on March 4, 1861, Lincoln said it was up to the South to decide if there would be war; at the end, he said: "We are not enemies but friends. We must not be enemies."

Lincoln moved very slowly at first. He waited for **Unionist sentiments**, or support for the Union, to develop in **Border States** like Delaware, Maryland, Kentucky, and Missouri. His lack of action caused even Cabinet members to wonder if he was up to the job. The South was also waiting, hopeful that Lincoln would surrender Fort Sumter without a fight and let the South leave the Union without a war.

Attack on Fort Sumter

Patience was wearing thin on both sides, and the new Confederate president, Jefferson Davis, feared that South Carolina would soon act on its own unless he pressured Anderson to leave Fort Sumter. On April 10, 1861, President Davis sent General P.G.T. Beauregard to demand the fort's surrender. On April 12, Beauregard sent officers to the fort, and Anderson told them he would run out of supplies in a few days unless he was resupplied. Beauregard seized the opportunity and told Anderson firing would begin on the fort in one hour. At 4:30 a.m., shelling began and continued for more than 30 long hours. Anderson surrendered the fort on April 14, and he and his men were allowed to leave by ship. The Civil War had begun.

Lincoln Calls for Volunteers

On April 15, President Lincoln ordered a naval blockade of all Southern ports and called on governors to supply 75,000 militia volunteers to put down the rebellion and save the Union. A **naval blockade** uses ships to block other ships from delivering supplies, troops, information, or aid to the opposing force.

Following Lincoln's call for volunteers, four more Southern states left the Union: Virginia, Arkansas, North Carolina, and Tennessee. The Confederacy had grown from seven to eleven states. However, Unionists convinced the Border States to remain in the Union.

Attack on Fort Sumter

Abraham Lincoln is elected president of the Union of the United States of America.

Results

Jefferson Davis is selected as president of the Confederate States of America.

Results

The Confederates attack Fort Sumter.

Results

President Lincoln calls for 75,000 volunteers.

Results

Student Instructions: Early Years of the War

Materials Needed

Glue, scissors, colored pencils

How to Create a Right-hand Interactive Notebook Page

Read the Key Details page. Then cut out the page and attach it to the right-hand page of your interactive notebook. Use what you have learned to create the left-hand page.

How to Create a Left-hand Interactive Notebook Page

Complete the following steps to create the left-hand page of your interactive notebook. Use lots of color.

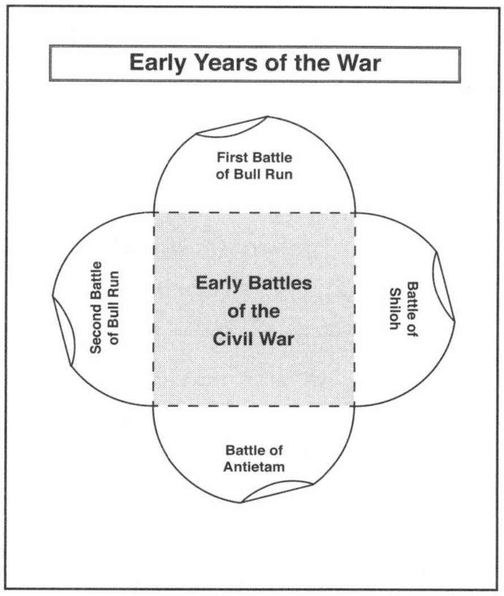

Step 1: Cut out the title and glue it to the top of the notebook page.

Step 2: Cut out the *Early Battles of the Civil War* flap book. Apply glue to the back of the gray center section and attach it below the title.

Step 3: Under each flap, write the date and results of the battle.

Demonstrate and Reflect on What You Have Learned

Early Years of the War

First Battle of Bull Run

Second Battle of Bull Run

Early Battles of the Civil War

Battle of Shiloh

Battle of Antietam

After the Battle of Fort Sumter in April of 1861, the conflict between the North and the South intensified. Many more battles were fought during the early part of the war. Use the Internet or other reference sources to complete the chart. Cut out the chart and glue it in your interactive notebook.

Battle	Date	State	Outcome
Battle of Wilson's Creek			
The Capture of Fort Donelson			
Battle of Belmont			
Seven Days Battle			

Key Details

Early Years of the War

Americans in the northern and southern states fought against each other in the Civil War. Both sides expected a quick end to the war. Instead, the war dragged on for four long years from April 12, 1861 to April 9, 1865.

Each side entered the war with different goals. The main goal of the North was to bring the Southern states back into the Union. At first, ending slavery was not a goal. The South had two goals: win recognition as an independent nation, the Confederate States of America, and to preserve slavery.

From the beginning, the Union forces outnumbered the Confederate forces. By the summer of 1861, the Union had about 187,000 soldiers. They were sometimes called Yankees. The Confederate Army had about 112,000 soldiers. They were also known as Rebels. By the end of the war, about 1 million men had fought for the South and over 2 million men had fought for the North, including thousands of African-American and Hispanic soldiers.

Major Battles

- **First Battle of Bull Run:** The first major battle of the Civil War was fought in July of 1861, at a small stream named Bull Run near Manassas, Virginia, a Confederate state. That fight took place a few miles from Washington, D.C., the capital of the Union States. Confederate troops under the command of General Pierce G.T. Beauregard forced the Union troops of General Irvin McDowell to retreat. Northern civilians who had ridden out to see the fight were  forced to flee with the Union troops to Washington, D.C. During the conflict, Confederate General Thomas J. Jackson earned the name "Stonewall Jackson" for holding his ground during the battle.

- **Battle of Shiloh:** The battle took place in Tennessee from April 6 to April 7, 1862. The battle began when the Confederate Army led by General Albert Sidney Johnston launched a surprise attack on Union troops under the command of General Ulysses S. Grant. On the second day, Union reinforcements forced Confederate troops back to the Mississippi River, resulting in a Union victory.

- **Second Battle of Bull Run:** This battle was fought from August 29 to August 30, 1862, on almost the same battlefield as the first Bull Run battle. Confederate troops led by General Robert E. Lee defeated Union troops led by General John Pope. President Lincoln fired Pope after the defeat.

- **Battle of Antietam:** This battle was fought in Sharpsburg, Maryland, near Antietam Creek on September 17, 1862. Confederate troops led by General Robert E. Lee fought Union troops led by General George B. McClellan. It was the first battle of the war to take place in a Union state. Eventually, Lee withdrew his force from the battlefield. The battle was counted as a victory for the Union, but casualties were high on both sides. There were nearly 23,000 total casualties, with over 3,600 killed. It is still the single bloodiest day in the history of the U.S. armed forces.

Early Years of the War

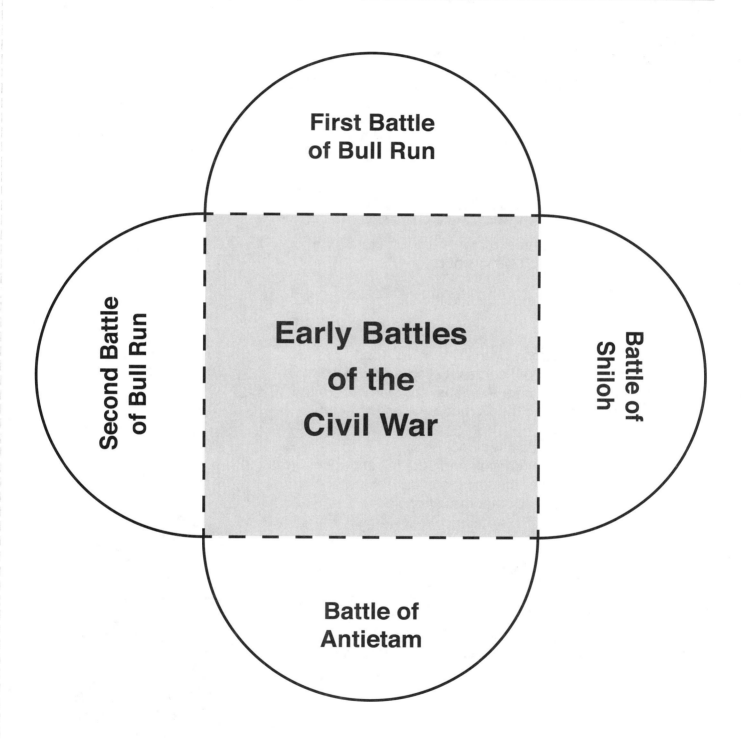

First Battle of Bull Run

Second Battle of Bull Run

Early Battles of the Civil War

Battle of Shiloh

Battle of Antietam

Student Instructions: War by Air and Sea

Materials Needed

Glue, scissors, colored pencils

How to Create a Right-hand Interactive Notebook Page

Read the Key Details page. Then cut out the page and attach it to the right-hand page of your interactive notebook. Use what you have learned to create the left-hand page.

How to Create a Left-hand Interactive Notebook Page

Complete the following steps to create the left-hand page of your interactive notebook. Use lots of color.

Step 1: Cut out the title and glue it to the top of the notebook page.

Step 2: Cut out the *Balloon Corps* flap book. Apply glue to the back of the gray center section and attach it below the title. Under the flaps, compare the Union balloon corps and the Confederate balloon corps.

Step 3: Cut out the *Ironclad* flap book. Apply glue to the back of the gray center section and attach it at the bottom of the page. Under the flaps, compare the Union ironclads and the Confederate ironclads.

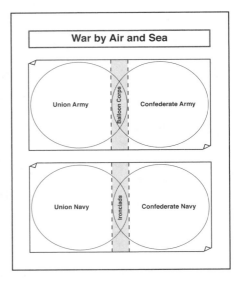

Demonstrate and Reflect on What You Have Learned

Think about what you learned from the reading selection. How do you think the use of balloons gave the North an advantage? Write the answer in your interactive notebook. Support your answer with specific details or examples.

Prof. Thaddeus S. Lowe replenishing the balloon *INTREPID* from the balloon *CONSTITUTION* – May 1862 – Fair Oaks, Virginia.

Key Details

War by Air and Sea

The Civil War was fought during an era of innovative technology and new inventions. Some of these innovations such as observation balloons and ironclad ships changed warfare forever.

Balloon Corps

Lighter-than-air balloons were used by both the Union and Confederate armies. The balloon was tethered to the ground and floated in the air. It was controlled by a person called an **aeronaut**. Balloons were used for **aerial surveillance** and provided information about enemy troop movements, numbers, and locations.

In 1861, President Lincoln named Thaddeus Lowe Chief Aeronaut of the Army of the Potomac. Lowe recruited and managed the North's first **balloon corps** (pronounced *kor*), The North had seven balloons made from white silk covered in varnish. Hydrogen gas was used to inflate the balloons.

In the Spring of 1862, Confederate Captain John Randolph Bryan developed the first of two balloons used in the war. The Confederates lacked the technology and resources of the Union Army, so the balloon was made of varnished cotton and inflated with air heated by burning pine knots and turpentine. Cotton was not a satisfactory material for hot-air balloons, but the cost of silk, the best material, was too expensive. Captain Langdon Cheves constructed the second balloon and overcame this problem by sewing together pieces of silk from dresses donated by Southern women to make a balloon.

The Ironclads

Union ships patrolled the Atlantic coast and the Gulf of Mexico, blocking Confederate trade routes. This prevented the South from receiving supplies or sending cotton, tobacco, and other trade goods to be sold.

In July 1861, Stephen Mallory, Confederate Secretary of the Navy, decided the South needed an ironclad ship to protect their coastline. **Ironclads** were wooden ships covered in iron plates. These ships were harder to destroy than the ships made only of wood. They raised the **USS *Merrimac***, a Union ship that had been sunk at the beginning of the war to prevent it from falling into Confederate hands. They covered the ship with iron plating and renamed it the **CSS *Virginia***. In October 1861, the North began construction of their own ironclad ship, the **USS *Monitor***.

USS* Monitor *(left) and CSS* Virginia *(right)

On March 9, 1862, the first battle of the ironclads was fought to a draw off the coast of Hampton Roads, Virginia. Only 50 yards apart at times, the two ironclads blasted cannonballs at each other. After a four-hour battle, the *Monitor* headed for water too shallow for the *Virginia* to follow. The *Virginia* returned to port for repairs.

The South eventually built 22 ironclad ships, but the North built more than 60. With their superior numbers, the Union tightened the blockade, captured most of the major ports in the South, and controlled inland rivers.

War by Air and Sea

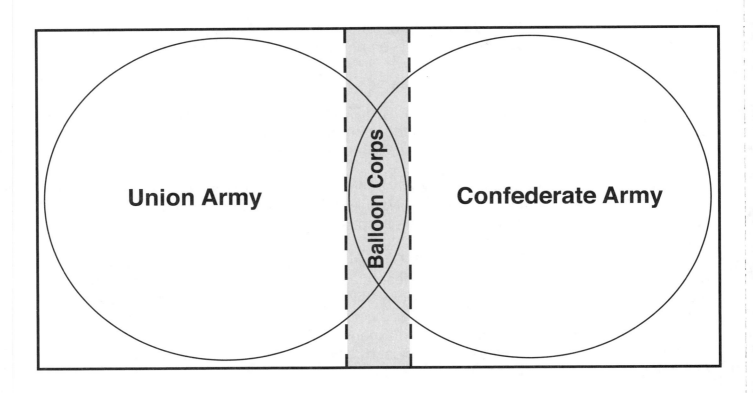

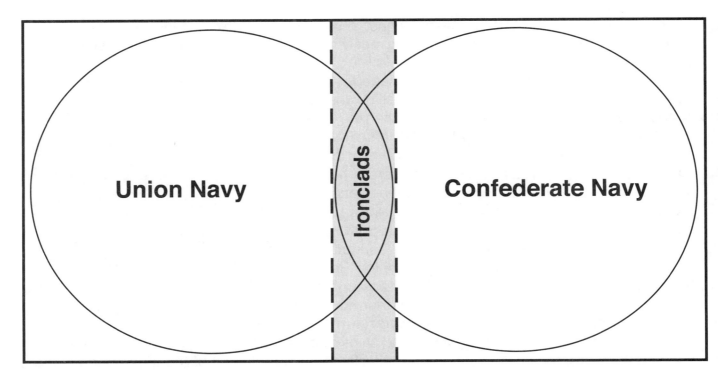

Student Instructions: Emancipation Proclamation

Materials Needed

Glue, scissors, colored pencils

How to Create a Right-hand Interactive Notebook Page

Read the Key Details page. Then cut out the page and attach it to the right-hand page of your interactive notebook. Use what you have learned to create the left-hand page.

How to Create a Left-hand Interactive Notebook Page

Complete the following steps to create the left-hand page of your interactive notebook. Use lots of color.

Step 1: Cut out the title and glue it to the top of the notebook page.

Step 2: Complete the four *Critical Details* pieces. Cut out each piece. Apply glue to the backs and attach them below the title.

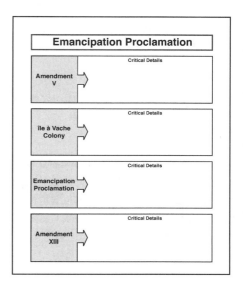

Demonstrate and Reflect on What You Have Learned

Examine a transcript of the Emancipation Proclamation at <https://www.archives.gov/exhibits/featured-documents/emancipation-proclamation/transcript.html>. According to the proclamation, what actions were to be required of the United States military and naval authority? Write the answer in your interactive notebook.

Key Details

Emancipation Proclamation

One of the most troubling questions of the Civil War was whether enslaved people should be freed, and when it should be done. In the early stages of the war, Congress said that the purpose of the war was to save the Union, not end slavery. That view was very close to President Lincoln's. In August 1862, he answered criticism from Horace Greeley, editor of the New York *Tribune*. Lincoln replied that regardless of his personal wish that slavery end, "My paramount object in this struggle is to save the Union and is not either to save or to destroy slavery." Lincoln's problem was that loyal border states like Missouri, Kentucky, and Maryland still had slaves; he could not risk stirring up more opposition in those states.

Colony on the Island of Île à Vache

Northern opinion at the time was as divided as it could possibly be. The old **abolitionists**, or people against slavery, were sure that freeing enslaved people was right. Others wanted to free the slaves but send them to Africa or Central America. Most Black people opposed this idea, and one, Robert Purvis, bluntly told Lincoln: "Sir, this is our country as much as it is yours, and we will not leave it." Despite protests from free Black people and abolitionists, President Lincoln tried to establish a colony on an island off the coast of Haiti called **Île à Vache**. It was a miserable failure, and after many of the "colonists" became ill, the survivors were brought back to the United States.

Emancipation Proclamation

There were some legal questions about freeing enslaved people in loyal states. **Amendment V** of the Constitution says that private property cannot be taken without just compensation. Enslaved people were considered private property. Lincoln offered a deal to border state leaders: free the enslaved people in your state, and the government will pay $400 for each one. They turned him down flat. If he could not persuade loyal border states to free enslaved people, he decided to justify freeing the enslaved people in Confederate states as a war measure.

On January 1, 1863, President Lincoln issued the **Emancipation Proclamation**, which freed enslaved people in all states still at war with the United States. The executive order freed about one million enslaved people. It did not apply to the three million people enslaved in states that had not seceded from the Union. The Confederacy ignored the order. Enslaved people remained slaves.

Lincoln knew that most slave owners would not willingly free their slaves, but he did not want to encourage enslaved people to revolt or to use violence if it could be avoided. In the words of Lincoln:

"...I hereby enjoin upon the people so declared to be free to abstain from all violence, unless in necessary self-defense; and I recommend to them that, in all cases when allowed, they labor faithfully for reasonable wages."

It wasn't until after the Civil War ended and the Thirteenth Amendment passed in 1865, that slavery was officially abolished everywhere in the United States.

Emancipation Proclamation

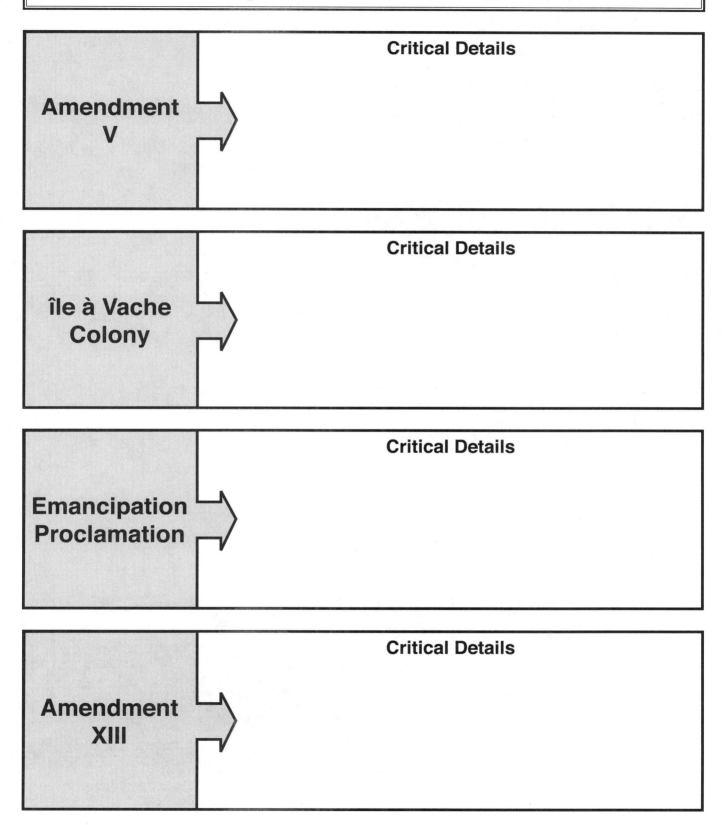

Amendment V

Critical Details

île à Vache Colony

Critical Details

Emancipation Proclamation

Critical Details

Amendment XIII

Critical Details

Student Instructions: Black Soldiers in the Civil War

Materials Needed

Glue, scissors, colored pencils

How to Create a Right-hand Interactive Notebook Page

Read the Key Details page. Then cut out the page and attach it to the right-hand page of your interactive notebook. Use what you have learned to create the left-hand page.

How to Create a Left-hand Interactive Notebook Page

Complete the following steps to create the left-hand page of your interactive notebook. Use lots of color.

Step 1: Cut out the title and glue it to the top of the notebook page.

Step 2: Complete the *Timeline* chart. Fill in the event for each date. Cut out the chart. Apply glue to the back and attach it below the title.

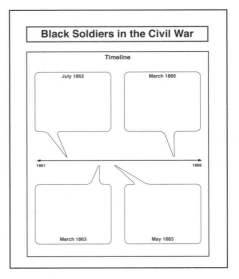

Demonstrate and Reflect on What You Have Learned

Learn more about Black soldiers in the Civil War. Go online to <nahttps://www.battlefields.org/learn/videos/black-soldiers-civil-war>. View the video *The Civil War in Four Minutes: Black Soldiers*. In your interactive notebook summarize what you learned.

Black soldiers of Company E, 4th U.S. Colored Infantry, at Fort Lincoln, District of Columbia

Key Details

Black Soldiers in the Civil War

Black soldiers had fought in the Revolutionary War and in the War of 1812, but when they first volunteered to fight in the Civil War, they were refused. Lincoln opposed the idea. He believed the enlistment of Black soldiers would cause the border states to reject the Union cause. However, by early 1862, President Lincoln was ready to accept Black men into the Union Army.

Militia Act of 1862

Although abolitionists urged President Lincoln to accept Black men as soldiers, the majority of politicians opposed the idea, believing that Black men could not learn the duties and become good soldiers. Frederick Douglass, who had escaped slavery, questioned this decision. "Why does the government reject the Negro? Is he not a man? Can he not wield a sword, fire a gun, march and countermarch, and obey orders like any other?" Finally, after more than a year of war, Congress passed the **Militia Act of July 1862**, allowing the president to employ Black men "for any military or naval service for which they may be found competent."

Black Soldiers in the Union Army

The **54th Massachusetts Volunteers** was activated on March 13, 1863. Black soldiers received only $10 a month as salary, $3 less than white soldiers. Black soldiers were not permitted to hold a rank higher than captain. Black regiments were led by white officers, and less than 100 Black men ever became officers. Their enthusiasm ran high, though in battle they often suffered high casualties.

The **Bureau of Colored Troops** was created by the United States War Department on May 22, 1863, to handle "all matters relating to the organization of colored troops." General Lorenzo Thomas was sent to the Mississippi Valley to recruit Black men. He was able to raise 76,000 soldiers—the first Black Union regiment.

Union regiments of Black soldiers fighting in South Carolina consisted mostly of those who

Recruiting poster for Black soldiers

were formerly enslaved, men who knew the territory and men who had strong motives to fight against their former owners for the freedom of their fellow slaves. At first, they were assigned only to menial tasks like cleaning latrines and building roads. Before the war ended, however, more than 186,000 Black soldiers fought in the Union Army and participated in over 400 battles.

Black Soldiers in the Confederate Army

Faced with a critical shortage of manpower, Jefferson Davis signed the **Negro Soldier Law** on March 13, 1865. Units of Black soldiers were organized in Richmond. Southern crowds threw mud and stones at the soldiers as they trained. However, the war ended soon after, and the Confederate Black soldiers never fought in the Civil War.

Black Soldiers in the Civil War

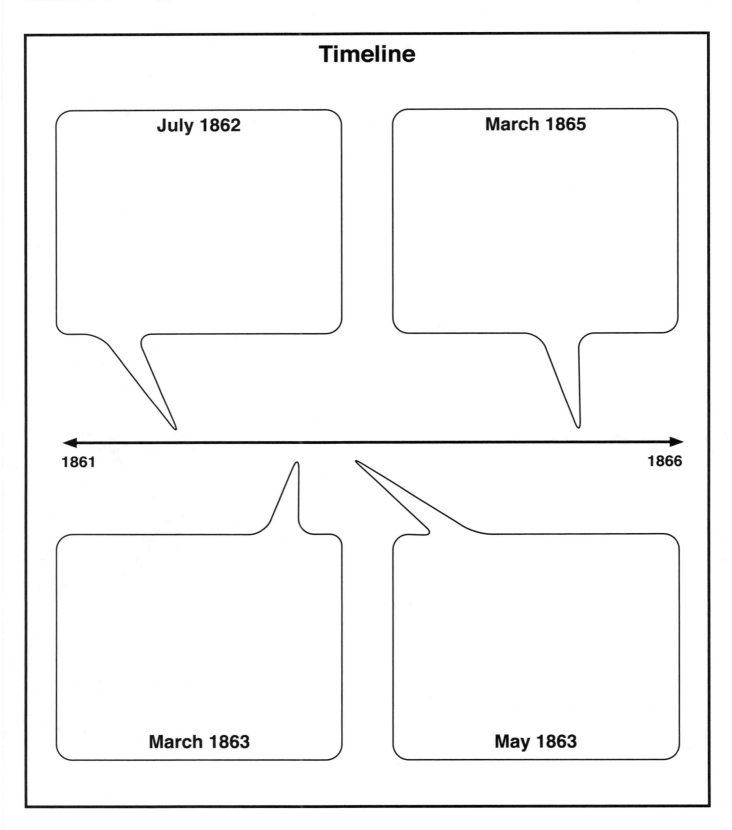

Student Instructions: Women and the Civil War

Materials Needed

Glue, scissors, colored pencils

How to Create a Right-hand Interactive Notebook Page

Read the Key Details page. Then cut out the page and attach it to the right-hand page of your interactive notebook. Use what you have learned to create the left-hand page.

How to Create a Left-hand Interactive Notebook Page

Complete the following steps to create the left-hand page of your interactive notebook. Use lots of color.

Step 1: Cut out the title and glue it to the top of the notebook page.

Step 2: Complete the *Women on the Home Front, Women Spies,* and *Women Serve as Nurses* pieces. Cut out the three pieces. Apply glue to the backs and attach them below the title.

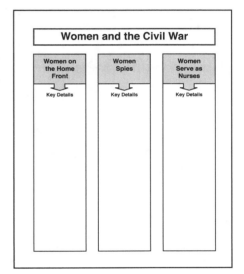

Demonstrate and Reflect on What You Have Learned

　　Known from a young age as "Wild Rose," Rose O'Neal Greenhow became the leader of a group of anti-Union spies. Use the Internet or other reference sources to research this famous Confederate sympathizer. In your interactive notebook, summarize her life as a spy.

Rose O'Neal Greenhow with her daughter in the Old Capitol Prison in Washington, D.C.

Key Details

Women and the Civil War

Women made important contributions to the war effort in both the North and the South.

*Mary "Mother" Bickerdyke,
Civil War nurse*

Women on the Home Front

Women were not supposed to be part of the war, but they were as patriotic and enthusiastic as the men. Before this time, it had not been proper for a "lady" to do much of the work that was now necessary. Women took over the farms, doing the chores their husbands had always done. Many went to work in factories to produce arms and clothing needed by the armies.

Women Spies

Some women became active participants in the war. Women spies were used by both sides, and some became famous. Rose Greenhow lived in Washington, D.C., and knew many government officials. She sent Confederate General Beauregard word that the Union Army was moving toward Bull Run. She was captured and held prisoner for a while. Belle Boyd often went through Union lines carrying information to General Stonewall Jackson and medicine for his troops. She was arrested six times and put in prison twice. During the war, many other women reported Union troop movements to Confederate officers.

Of Northern spies, the most important was Elizabeth Van Lew, who lived in Richmond and gathered information from Union prisoners held at Libby Prison. She was even able to plant one of her former slaves, Mary Bowser, as a servant at President Jefferson Davis's home. Her information to General Grant was extremely useful. When his army entered Richmond, the Confederate capital, he stopped at her home for tea. Harriet Tubman also served the Union Army. She worked as a cook, spy, nurse, and scout.

A few women even disguised themselves as men and enlisted in the army.

Women Serve as Nurses

Nursing wounded soldiers was a common activity among Southern women during the war. Because the South was short on medical supplies, food, and doctors, women were crucial in the saving of many lives. After a battle, homes in the area became field hospitals for wounded and sick soldiers.

Several Northern women played a major role in nursing during the war. Dorothea Dix was Superintendent of the United States Army Nurses, with a rank equal to that of a major general. When she saw the needs of soldiers, she issued appeals for bed shirts, preserves, and canned goods. Clara Barton became famous as a battlefield nurse. She aided soldiers and civilians during the war. She later founded the **American Red Cross**. Mary "Mother" Bickerdyke was a widow in her forties who devoted great efforts to taking care of enlisted men. General Grant and General Sherman admired her efforts.

Women and the Civil War

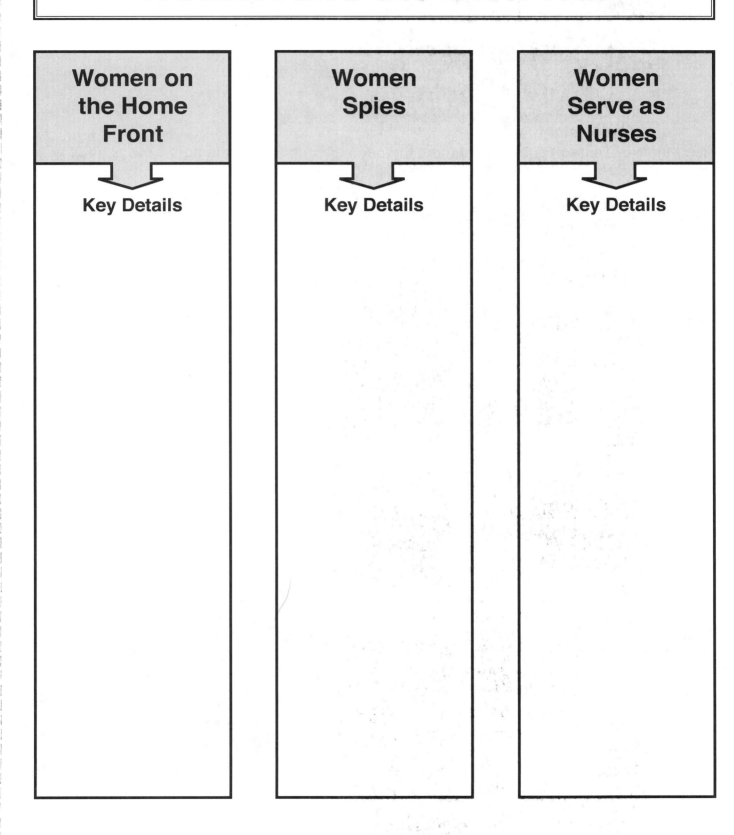

Women on the Home Front	Women Spies	Women Serve as Nurses
Key Details	Key Details	Key Details

Student Instructions: Lincoln Struggles to Find a General

Materials Needed

Glue, scissors, colored pencils

How to Create a Right-hand Interactive Notebook Page

Read the Key Details page. Then cut out the page and attach it to the right-hand page of your interactive notebook. Use what you have learned to create the left-hand page.

How to Create a Left-hand Interactive Notebook Page

Complete the following steps to create the left-hand page of your interactive notebook. Use lots of color.

Step 1: Cut out the title and glue it to the top of the notebook page.

Step 2: Complete the two puzzle pieces. Cut out the pieces. Apply glue to the backs and attach them below the title.

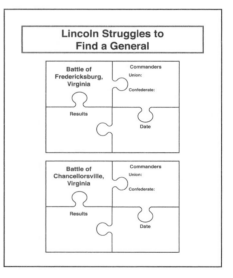

Demonstrate and Reflect on What You Have Learned

General Ambrose Burnside, Commander of the Army of the Potomac, devised a plan to take Fredericksburg, Virginia, on the Rappahannock River. On the other side, General Robert E Lee and 78,000 Confederate troops waited. Research the Battle of Fredericksburg. How did General Burnside cross the Rappahannock? Write the answer in your interactive notebook. Support your answer with specific details or examples.

Battle of Fredericksburg

Key Details

Lincoln Struggles to Find a General

General Robert E. Lee and the Confederate Army of Northern Virginia seemed unbeatable during the winter months of 1862 to 1863. President Lincoln struggled to find a winning general to lead the Union Army and defeat Lee.

Battle of Fredericksburg

President Lincoln fired General McClellan as commander of the Army of the Potomac after McClellan did not hand a crippling defeat to the Confederate Army at the Battle of Antietam in 1862. Lincoln replaced McClellan with General Ambrose Burnside.

A goal of the Union since the war began in the spring of 1861 had been to capture the Confederate capital at Richmond, Virginia. It was a vital source of weapons and supplies for the Confederate Army. General Burnside devised a plan to take Fredericksburg, Virginia, on the Rappahannock River then drive on to Richmond and capture the city.

General Ambrose Burnside

On December 13, 1862, the Union attacked the Confederate troops dug in on several hills south of town. It was the largest battle of the Civil War. It involved more soldiers than any other battle during the war. The Confederate Army had been rebuilt since Antietam. Lee now had 78,000 men in two corps under the leadership of General Stonewall Jackson and General James Longstreet. The Union Army under Burnside's leadership consisted of 123,000 men led by three generals: Edwin Sumner, Joe Hooker, and William Franklin. Repeated attacks by Union troops failed to overcome Lee's troops. Burnside's failure cost him his job, and 12,500 of his men lost their lives or were severely wounded.

Battle of Chancellorsville

After General Burnside's crushing defeat at Fredericksburg in 1862, President Lincoln again searched for a general to lead the Army of the Potomac. In January 1863, he chose General Joseph Hooker for the job.

Hooker rebuilt the Union Army and devised a plan to take the Confederate capital. Lee and the Confederates were still near Fredericksburg guarding the way to Richmond. Hooker planned to launch an attack on Lee, forcing him to retreat, then march on to Richmond, Virginia, and take the city.

On April 30, 1863, Hooker sent his force of 97,000 to surround Lee near Fredericksburg. Under attack, Lee split his army of 57,000 men into two forces. He sent half of his soldiers, led by General Stonewall Jackson, to attack Hooker's army at Chancellorsville, a few miles west of Fredericksburg. The Confederates continued to attack the Union Army over the next several days. The Union Army was forced to retreat on May 7, 1863.

Both sides suffered heavy **casualties** (killed, wounded, or captured). The Confederate Army lost over 13,000 men. They also lost a general when Stonewall Jackson was accidentally shot by his own men. The Union suffered over 17,000 casualties. The Union defeat at the Battle of Chancellorsville led Hooker to resign as commander of the Army of the Potomac.

Lincoln Struggles to Find a General

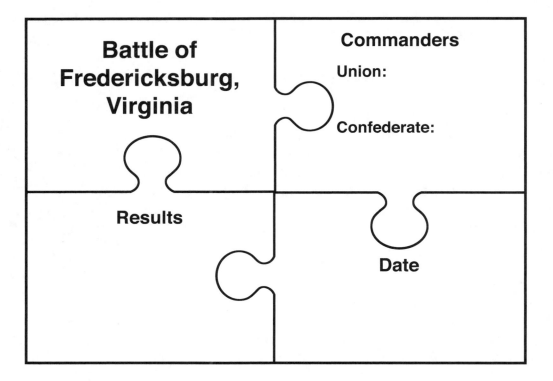

Battle of Fredericksburg, Virginia

Commanders

Union:

Confederate:

Results

Date

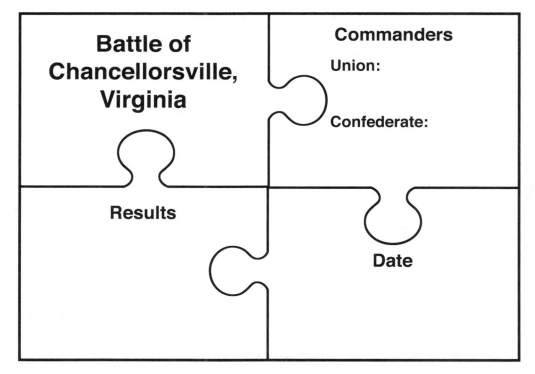

Battle of Chancellorsville, Virginia

Commanders

Union:

Confederate:

Results

Date

Student Instructions: Northern Victories Turn the War

Materials Needed

Glue, scissors, colored pencils

How to Create a Right-hand Interactive Notebook Page

Read the Key Details page. Then cut out the page and attach it to the right-hand page of your interactive notebook. Use what you have learned to create the left-hand page.

How to Create a Left-hand Interactive Notebook Page

Complete the following steps to create the left-hand page of your interactive notebook. Use lots of color.

Step 1: Cut out the title and glue it to the top of the notebook page.

Step 2: Cut out the *Definition* flap book. Apply glue to the back of the gray tab and attach it below the title. Under each flap explain the term.

Step 3: Complete the *Civil War States* map. Color the Union States blue. Color the Confederate states red. Place stars on the map indicating the location of the Battle of Vicksburg and the Battle of Gettysburg. Write the name of the battle by the correct star. If you need help, use the Internet or other reference sources.

Step 4: Cut out the *Civil War States* flap book. Apply glue to the back of the map section and attach at the bottom of the page. Under each flap, explain the importance of the battle.

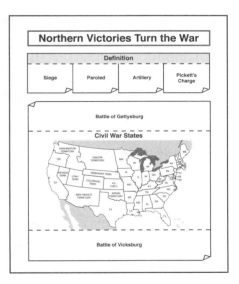

Demonstrate and Reflect on What You Have Learned

President Lincoln was invited to speak at the dedication of a cemetery in Gettysburg, Pennsylvania, on November 19, 1863. Lincoln's speech lasted less than two minutes. Read a transcript of the speech at <https://www.ourdocuments.gov/doc.php?flash=false&doc=36&page=transcript>. Why do you think the Gettysburg Address has become one of the best-remembered speeches in American history? Write the answer in your interactive notebook. Support your opinion with specific details and examples.

**President Abraham Lincoln
in November 1863**

Key Details

Northern Victories Turn the War

President Lincoln was frustrated with Union military leadership during the first two years of the war. He was desperate to find generals who could defeat General Robert E. Lee and the Confederate Army.

Victory at Vicksburg

Vicksburg, Mississippi, the last Confederate stronghold on the Mississippi River, sat comfortably on a high bluff overlooking the river with marshy lowlands to the west. Vicksburg connected Texas, Arkansas, and Louisiana with the rest of the Confederacy. One of the main goals of the Union was to gain control of the river.

General Ulysses S. Grant's troops surrounded the city, cutting off essential supplies on May 25, 1863. In the long **siege**, the city became primitive. Shelling made it unsafe to live in houses, so the citizens dug caves in the bluffs for shelter. Food was in short supply, and people ate horses, mules, dogs, cats, and muskrats. Due to the low food supply and the possibility that Union forces would make a strong attack, Confederate general John Clifford Pemberton surrendered Vicksburg on July 4, 1863. Pemberton arranged with Grant for his troops to be **paroled**, or released, rather than sent to a prison camp. The battle was a great victory for Grant. His forces captured 31,600 soldiers, 172 cannons, 60,000 muskets, and a large supply of ammunition. It gave control of the Mississippi River to the Union.

Victory at Gettysburg

The battle at Gettysburg, Pennsylvania, was the turning point of the Civil War. Confederate general Robert E. Lee's plan to invade the North and force an immediate end to the war failed. The conflict took place over a three-day period near the small town of Gettysburg. On July 1, 1863, the first day of the battle, the two armies met in the fields west of Gettysburg. The Confederate Army outnumbered the Union Army, and after a full day of fighting, the Union retreated to Cemetery Hill.

When Union general George Gordon Meade arrived on July 2, he found the Union Army dug in on top of Cemetery Hill and Seminary Ridge. Unknown to Lee, the 94,000 Union troops now outnumbered the 72,000 Confederate troops. Lee launched an attack. The fighting was fierce, and both sides suffered heavy causalities. It was all in vain, however, as Union troops managed to hold them back.

The last battle began on July 3 when 140 Confederate cannons opened fire and 118 Union cannons responded. The **artillery**, or cannons, went at each other for two hours. Running low on ammunition, General George Edward Pickett's 6,000 Confederate soldiers formed in three ranks as if on parade and led a charge of about 15,000 total Confederates. Remembered as **Pickett's Charge**, they moved forward at 110 paces a minute across a mile of open ground. The Union fired everything available at them, but the Rebel wave kept coming, and some reached the Yankee line before being killed or captured. It had been a heroic effort, but a dismal failure. About half of Pickett's men were killed, wounded, or captured in the charge.

Total casualties for both sides for the Battle of Gettysburg were approximately 7,000 killed, 33,000 wounded, and 11,000 missing or captured. Losses were fairly even, but on July 4, the Confederates began to withdraw.

Northern Victories Turn the War

Definition

Siege	Paroled	Artillery	Pickett's Charge

Battle of Gettysburg

Civil War States

Battle of Vicksburg

Student Instructions: Presidential Election of 1864

Materials Needed

Glue, scissors, colored pencils

How to Create a Right-hand Interactive Notebook Page

Read the Key Details page. Then cut out the page and attach it to the right-hand page of your interactive notebook. Use what you have learned to create the left-hand page.

How to Create a Left-hand Interactive Notebook Page

Complete the following steps to create the left-hand page of your interactive notebook. Use lots of color.

Step 1: Cut out the title and glue it to the top of the notebook page.

Step 2: Complete the *Lincoln vs. McClellan* chart. Cut out the chart. Apply glue to the back of the gray center section and attach it below the title.

Step 3: Under each flap, record the election outcome. The *Problems for the Candidate* can also be continued under each flap, if needed.

Demonstrate and Reflect on What You Have Learned

In the 1864 presidential election, President Abraham Lincoln's opponent was Major General George McClellan. At the beginning of the Civil War, McClellan held the position of commander of the Army of the Potomac and later general-in-chief of all armies of the United States. Lincoln eventually removed McClellan from both positions. Use the Internet or other reference resources to research the career of the general. Why was McClellan fired twice by Lincoln? Write the answer in your interactive notebook. Support your answer with details or examples.

President Lincoln visits General McClellan at Antietam, Maryland, in October 1862.

Key Details

Presidential Election of 1864

The election of 1864 took place in the middle of the Civil War. Only the 25 states still in the Union participated, the 11 Confederate states did not.

The Democratic Presidential Candidate

General George B. McClellan and President Abraham Lincoln did not get along. At the beginning of the war, McClellan held the position of commander of the Army of the Potomac, and later general-in-chief of all armies of the United States. Unhappy with his leadership, Lincoln finally removed McClellan from both positions. When no further military orders came for him, McClellan became a politician and ran against Lincoln in the 1864 election. He resigned his commission in the army on election day.

The Democratic convention was held in Chicago, and its delegates were split between two groups. The **War Democrats** supported the war. The **Peace Democrats** were opponents of the war. The Democratic Peace group chose George B. McClellan as their presidential candidate. His running mate was George Pendleton. McClellan ran on an anti-Lincoln and anti-Emancipation Proclamation platform and left open the possibility of a negotiated peace with the South.

By November of 1864, a string of Union successes had convinced many that the war was in its final phase. McClellan's promise to immediately negotiate peace terms with the Confederacy did not sit well with Union soldiers.

The Republican Presidential Candidate

In 1864, President Lincoln faced many challenges. The war was now in its fourth year. Critics seemed almost everywhere. Senator Ben Wade bluntly told Lincoln: "You are the father of every military blunder that has been made during the war." Many battles had been lost: Bull Run, Fredericksburg, and Chancellorsville among them. Victories had been hard won at Antietam, Vicksburg, and Gettysburg. Brighter days might be ahead, but would voters forget the disasters of the past?

Meeting in Baltimore, the Republicans chose Lincoln for a second term, with Democrat Andrew Johnson for vice president. Lincoln said that the party had decided it was best not to "swap horses while crossing the river."

In an effort to broaden their support, the Republican Party chose to join with the War Democrats and called themselves the **National Union Party**. The National Union platform called for concluding the war with an unconditional Confederate surrender, an amendment to end slavery, and support for disabled veterans. If Lincoln were reelected, it would be the first time in over thirty years that an **incumbent president**, or a person holding the office of president before the election, won a second term.

Election Results

In electoral votes, Lincoln won 212. Lincoln won every state except for Kentucky, New Jersey, and Delaware. McClellan won 21 electoral votes.

Presidential Election of 1864

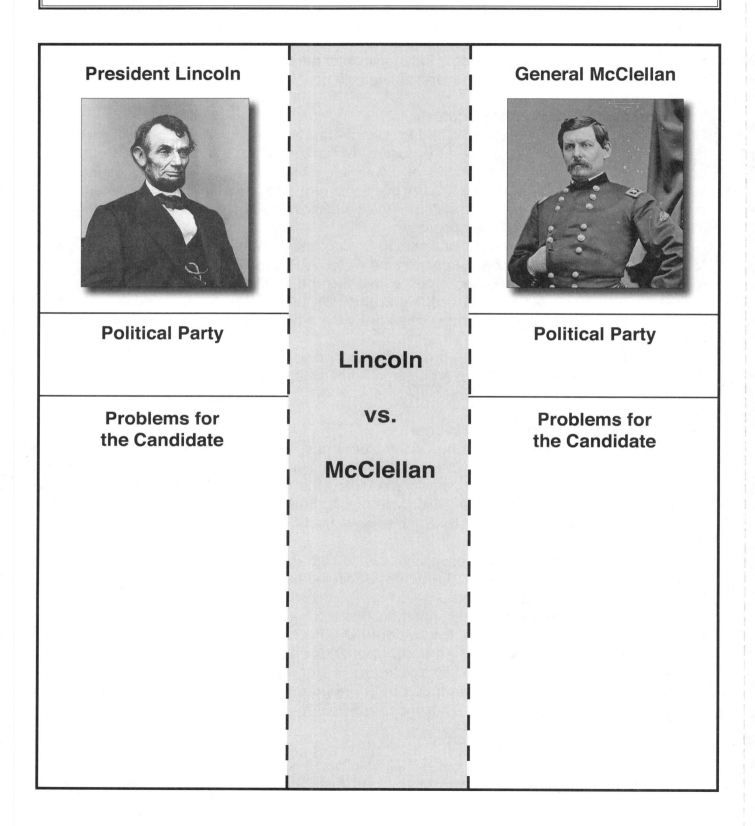

President Lincoln

Political Party

**Problems for
the Candidate**

Lincoln

vs.

McClellan

General McClellan

Political Party

**Problems for
the Candidate**

Student Instructions: Grant vs. Lee

Materials Needed

Glue, scissors, colored pencils

How to Create a Right-hand Interactive Notebook Page

Read the Key Details page. Then cut out the page and attach it to the right-hand page of your interactive notebook. Use what you have learned to create the left-hand page.

How to Create a Left-hand Interactive Notebook Page

Complete the following steps to create the left-hand page of your interactive notebook. Use lots of color.

Step 1: Cut out the title and glue it to the top of the notebook page.

Step 2: Cut out the *General Ulysses S. Grant* and *General Robert E. Lee* pockets. Fold back the gray tabs on the dotted lines. Apply glue to each of the gray tabs and attach the pockets below the title.

Step 3: Cut apart the word strips. Place each strip in the correct pocket.

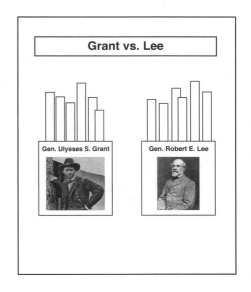

Demonstrate and Reflect on What You Have Learned

The United States Military Academy at West Point, New York, (also known as West Point) was established in 1806. Union general Ulysses S. Grant and Confederate general Robert E. Lee both graduated from the school. Use the Internet or other reference sources to research West Point. For what branch of the United States military does West Point provide higher education and training? Write the answer in your interactive notebook.

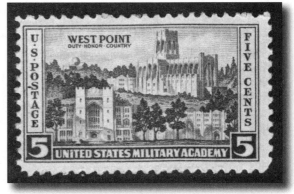

The West Point commemorative stamp was issued in 1937.

Key Details

Grant vs. Lee

Both North and South struggled to find generals who could lead armies into battle and win. The outcome of the war finally came down to the leadership of two men.

General Ulysses S. Grant

Ulysses S. Grant was born in 1822 in Ohio. He graduated from the United States Military Academy at West Point, New York, (also known as West Point). After graduating from West Point, Grant became an officer in the United States Army. He fought during the Mexican-American War (1846–1848). He was eventually forced to leave the Army, and he returned home and opened a general store.

With the start of the Civil War, Grant reentered the military. He started out with the Illinois militia and soon moved up the ranks in the Army to general. In 1862, Grant had his first major victory when he captured Fort Donelson in Tennessee. He became known as U.S. (Unconditional Surrender) Grant when he told the Confederate commanders "No terms except unconditional and immediate surrender."

Grant's victory at Fort Donelson was the first major victory for the Union during the Civil War. He went on to lead his army to victory at the battles of Shiloh, Vicksburg, and Chattanooga. In 1864, President Abraham Lincoln made Grant general-in-chief of the entire Union Army. Grant began his campaign to defeat Lee's forces and capture the Confederate capital of Richmond in Virginia. Grant then led the Union Army against Robert E. Lee in Virginia. They battled for over a year, with Grant eventually defeating Lee at Petersburg. Lee and the Confederate Army surrendered at Appomattox Court House, Virginia.

Northerners considered Grant a war hero. His popularity helped him get elected the 18th President of the United States in 1868. He served two terms as president.

General Robert Edward Lee

Robert E. Lee was born in 1807 in Virginia. He graduated second in his West Point class and served in the Mexican-American War. He went on to become a colonel in the U.S. 1st Cavalry. When the Civil War began in 1861, President Lincoln offered Lee command of the Union Army. Lee refused and resigned his command to serve in the South. By the end of the war, he was commander-in-chief of the Confederate Army.

Lee earned the nickname the "Gray Fox" because he wore the gray uniform of the Confederate soldier and rode a gray horse, and he was considered a smart and cunning military leader. Lee's first big victory over the North was the Seven Days Battle in Virginia. Other victories included the Battle of Chancellorsville, the Battle of Fredericksburg, and the Battle of Cold Harbor.

On April 9, 1865, General Robert E. Lee surrendered his army to General Ulysses S. Grant at the village of Appomattox Court House, Virginia. Although Lee could have been tried and hung as a traitor to the Union of the United States, he was **paroled** at the time of his surrender and allowed to return home, as were most soldiers in the Confederate Army. Lee later became president of Washington College in Lexington, Virginia. Although Lee signed the loyalty oath and applied for a **pardon**, his paperwork was misplaced. His pardon was granted and his citizenship rights were restored **posthumously** (after his death) on August 5, 1975.

Grant vs. Lee

General Ulysses S. Grant

General Robert E. Lee

Commander-in-chief of the Confederate Army
Commander-in-chief of the Union Army
Nicknamed "U.S." for "Unconditional Surrender"
Nicknamed the "Gray Fox"
First major victory was Fort Donelson
First major victory was the Seven Days Battle
Victories included Chancellorsville, Fredericksburg, and Cold Harbor
Victories included Vicksburg, Chattanooga, and Petersburg
Accepted surrender of Army of Northern Virginia at Appomattox Court House
Surrendered at Appomattox Court House, Virginia
President of Washington College in Lexington, Virginia
18th President of the United States

Student Instructions: Final Phase of the War

Materials Needed

Glue, scissors, colored pencils

How to Create a Right-hand Interactive Notebook Page

Read the Key Details page. Then cut out the page and attach it to the right-hand page of your interactive notebook. Use what you have learned to create the left-hand page.

How to Create a Left-hand Interactive Notebook Page

Complete the following steps to create the left-hand page of your interactive notebook. Use lots of color.

Step 1: Cut out the title and glue it to the top of the notebook page.

Step 2: Complete the *Civil War Battles* chart. Cut out the chart. Apply glue to the back of the chart and attach it below the title.

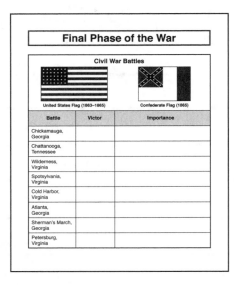

Demonstrate and Reflect on What You Have Learned

Use the Internet or other reference sources to research the Civil War. Label the Civil War Theaters on the map below. Color in the state with the most Civil War battles. Cut out the map and glue it in your interactive notebook.

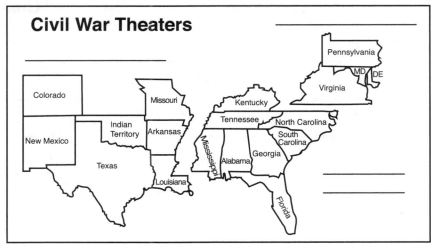

Final Phase of the War

The Civil War was fought in several areas of the United States called **theaters**. The **Eastern Theater** included the area east of the Appalachian Mountains. The **Western Theater** covered the area west of the Appalachians and east of the Mississippi River. The **Trans-Mississippi Theater** encompassed everything west of the Mississippi River.

Major Battles in the Final Phase of the War

The battle of Chickamauga, Georgia, was fought September 19–20, 1863. The Union forces led by Major General William S. Rosecrans and Major General George H. Thomas clashed with the Confederate Army led by General Braxton Bragg and Lt. General James Longstreet. The two-day conflict was the largest Confederate victory in the Western Theater.

The battle of Chattanooga, Tennessee, was fought November 23–25, 1863. The Union Army was led by General Ulysses S. Grant and the Confederate Army was led by General Braxton Bragg. The city of Chattanooga was a key Confederate railroad hub supplying Confederate troops. The battle was a victory for the North.

The Battle of the Wilderness was fought in Virginia May 5–7, 1864. It was the first battle of Union general Ulysses S. Grant's **Overland Campaign**, a plan to defeat Confederate general Robert E. Lee's army and capture the South's capital at Richmond, Virginia. The two-day battle was a draw; Union forces were unable to defeat the Confederate forces.

The battle of Spotsylvania, Virginia, was fought from May 8 to May 21, 1864. It was part of General Grant's Overland Campaign. As part of the plan, he had to capture the important crossroads of Spotsylvania Court House. The battle ended in a draw. Grant decided he could not defeat Lee, so he ordered the Union Army to move southward.

The battle of Cold Harbor, Virginia, was fought from May 31 to June 12, 1864. It was the continuation of Grant's plan to take the Confederate capital. The battle was a defeat for the Union Army and Lee's last major victory of the war.

The battle of Atlanta, Georgia, was fought from July 7 to September 2, 1864. After a two-month **siege** where Union troops surrounded and blocked supplies to the city, General William Tecumseh Sherman and Union troops captured Atlanta. The city was a major supply center of the Confederate states. Its loss proved to be a major blow to the Confederacy and led to the end of the Civil War.

General Sherman and his Union troops marched to Savannah, Georgia, in what became known as **Sherman's March to the Sea**. They took control of the seaport. His army destroyed and burned much of the land they passed through on the way. When Sherman arrived in Savannah, Confederate forces fled, and the mayor of Savannah surrendered the city.

The siege of Petersburg, Virginia, was conducted from July 20, 1864, to April 2, 1865. Grant wanted to capture this important railroad hub supplying Confederate troops. Grant's nearly year-long siege of the city ended in a Union victory. It was the last major battle of the American Civil War.

Sherman's men destroying the railroad in Atlanta, Georgia

Final Phase of the War

Civil War Battles

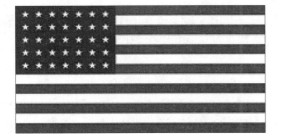

United States Flag (1863–1865)

Confederate Flag (1865)

Battle	Victor	Importance
Chickamauga, Georgia		
Chattanooga, Tennessee		
Wilderness, Virginia		
Spotsylvania, Virginia		
Cold Harbor, Virginia		
Atlanta, Georgia		
Sherman's March, Georgia		
Petersburg, Virginia		

Student Instructions: Surrender at Appomattox Court House

Materials Needed

Glue, scissors, colored pencils

How to Create a Right-hand Interactive Notebook Page

Read the Key Details page. Then cut out the page and attach it to the right-hand page of your interactive notebook. Use what you have learned to create the left-hand page.

How to Create a Left-hand Interactive Notebook Page

Complete the following steps to create the left-hand page of your interactive notebook. Use lots of color.

Step 1: Cut out the title and glue it to the top of the notebook page.

Step 2: Cut out each of the *Question* pieces. Apply glue to the back of each gray tab and attach them below the title.

Step 3: Under each flap, answer the question.

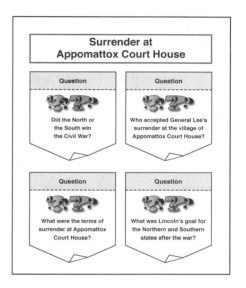

Demonstrate and Reflect on What You Have Learned

General Robert E. Lee arrived at the McLean house in the village of Appomattox Court House at one o'clock on April 9, 1865, and took a seat in the parlor. General Grant entered the house 30 minutes later. Use the Internet or other resources to research the meeting. Over the years, much has been made of the condition of each general's uniform. How did each general dress for the meeting? Write the answer in your interactive notebook. Support your answer with specified details or examples.

The surrender of General Lee to General Grant at Appomattox Court House, Virginia, on April 9, 1865

Key Details

Surrender at Appomattox Court House

Throughout the winter months of 1864 to 1865, the Union continued the **siege** of Petersburg, surrounding and blocking supplies to the city. The Confederate Army suffered heavy casualties defending Petersburg. General Robert E. Lee sent a message to President Davis that he was withdrawing troops from the city.

Cannons in the Union lines surrounding Petersburg, Virginia, during the months-long siege

Lee's Army on the Run

On April 2, 1865, Lee withdrew his troops from Petersburg and headed west to the village of Amelia Court House. On the same day, the Confederate government fled Richmond on Lee's recommendation. Both Petersburg, and then Richmond, the capital of the Confederacy, were captured by the Union. Union troops continued a running battle with the retreating troops.

General Grant realized that if he continued to push his advantage, there was a good chance that General Lee would surrender. President Lincoln agreed and gave the order to proceed.

For several days, Lee's men continued to fight as they fled west. The morning of April 9, 1865, Lee knew the war was over. The Army of Northern Virginia was outnumbered, out of supplies, and cut off from getting to Amelia Court House. General Lee felt he had no choice but to surrender and sent a message to Grant.

Confederate Army Surrenders

General Grant sent a message under a **flag of truce** offering to accept Lee's surrender. General Lee agreed. Grant ordered an immediate cease-fire.

On April 9, 1865, General Lee and his troops surrendered to Grant in the village of Appomattox Court House, Virginia. The men met in the front parlor of a two-story brick farmhouse owned by Wilmer McLean. Lee surrendered all men, arms, ammunition, and supplies except the horses and mules that were the personal property of the soldiers. Lee also offered to return about 1,000 Union soldiers who were prisoners of war because he had no food for them. Grant accepted his offer and then sent beef, bread, coffee, and sugar to feed the Confederate troops.

When Union soldiers began firing cannon salutes to celebrate the end of the war, General Grant ordered all loud celebrations ended. "The war is over, the rebels are our countrymen again," he told them.

More than 600,000 Americans died in the Civil War. Thousands more were wounded or left seriously ill. Over one-fifth of the adult white males in the South died. Men returned to their families blind, deaf, or missing arms and legs. Nearly 40,000 African Americans died while serving as Union soldiers or sailors.

Lincoln looked forward to "a just and lasting peace." His goal was to help both sides recover and rebuild. At his first public appearance after the war, Lincoln asked the band to play "Dixie," a favorite Southern song. "I have always thought 'Dixie' one of the best tunes I have ever heard," he said.

Surrender at Appomattox Court House

Question

Did the North or the South win the Civil War?

Question

Who accepted General Lee's surrender at the village of Appomattox Court House?

Question

What were the terms of surrender at Appomattox Court House?

Question

What was Lincoln's goal for the Northern and Southern states after the war?

Student Instructions: Impact of the Civil War

Materials Needed

Glue, scissors, colored pencils

How to Create a Right-hand Interactive Notebook Page

Read the Key Details page. Then cut out the page and attach it to the right-hand page of your interactive notebook. Use what you have learned to create the left-hand page.

How to Create a Left-hand Interactive Notebook Page

Complete the following steps to create the left-hand page of your interactive notebook. Use lots of color.

Step 1: Cut out the title and glue it to the top of the notebook page.

Step 2: Cut out the *Vocabulary* flap book. Apply glue to the back of the gray center section and attach it below the title. Under each flap, explain the term.

Step 3: Cut out the *Consequences of the Civil War* flap book. Cut on the solid lines to create four flaps. Apply glue to the back of the gray tab and attach it at the bottom of the page. Under each flap, write the consequence.

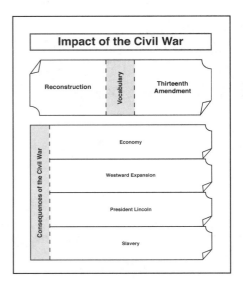

Demonstrate and Reflect on What You Have Learned

On April 14, 1865, President Lincoln was shot at Ford's Theatre. Go online to <https://digital.library.mcgill.ca/Lincoln/exhibit/text/Assassination.html> and read the journal entries of Dr. C. S. Taft who cared for Lincoln until his death. Use the Internet or other reference sources to research the assassination of Lincoln. Think about what you learned from Dr. Taft's journal and your research. From the perspective of an eyewitness, write several journal entries in your interactive notebook about the event. Each entry should include the date and specific details.

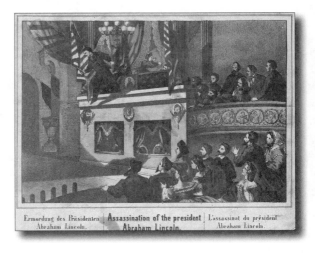

> **Key Details**

Impact of the Civil War

The Civil War lasted four years and was the most devastating war in American history, with over 600,000 military deaths. The fighting started at Fort Sumter in South Carolina on April 12, 1861. The major fighting of the war ended on April 9, 1865, at Wilmer McLean's house in the village of Appomattox Court House, Virginia. The terms of surrender were signed by Generals Robert E. Lee and Ulysses S. Grant. The Civil War saved the Union but changed the nation forever.

Economy of North and South

The Civil War caused billions of dollars of damage to the South. Towns and cities, large plantations, small farms, roads, bridges, and railroads were left in ruins. The destruction caused by the war forced the South to begin an era of **Reconstruction**, or rebuilding of the South's government, society, and infrastructure.

The ruins of Charleston, South Carolina

The Civil War changed northern industry. Small shops were replaced by large factories. Businessmen went from selling to local markets to national markets. Even in agriculture, the small farmer who tried to get by without expensive equipment was doomed to lose out to his neighbor who was equipped with the latest thresher, planter, or harvester.

Westward Expansion

The Civil War changed the course of westward expansion. In May 1862, Congress passed the **Homestead Act**, offering free land to homesteaders to encourage settlement of western territory. Congress also passed the **Pacific Railroad Act** in 1862. This law chartered two railroad companies to build a transcontinental railroad. In 1869, the Central Pacific and Union Pacific Railroads met at Promontory Summit, Utah, making transportation of people and goods from the Atlantic to the Pacific faster and easier.

Assassination of President Lincoln

Many Southerners blamed Abraham Lincoln for the Civil War. On April 14, 1865, President Lincoln was shot by Confederate sympathizer John Wilkes Booth while attending a play at Ford's Theatre in Washington, D.C. Booth escaped but was later tracked down and killed. Lincoln never regained consciousness and died the following morning.

Slavery

The war ended slavery. President Lincoln issued the **Emancipation Proclamation** on January 1, 1863. This document proclaimed that any enslaved people held in the rebellious states "are, and henceforward shall be free." Lincoln allowed Black soldiers to fight for the Union. Before his death, he supported the passage of the **Thirteenth Amendment** that would officially end slavery in the United States. The Thirteenth Amendment was ratified on December 6, 1865, approximately seven months after his death.

Impact of the Civil War

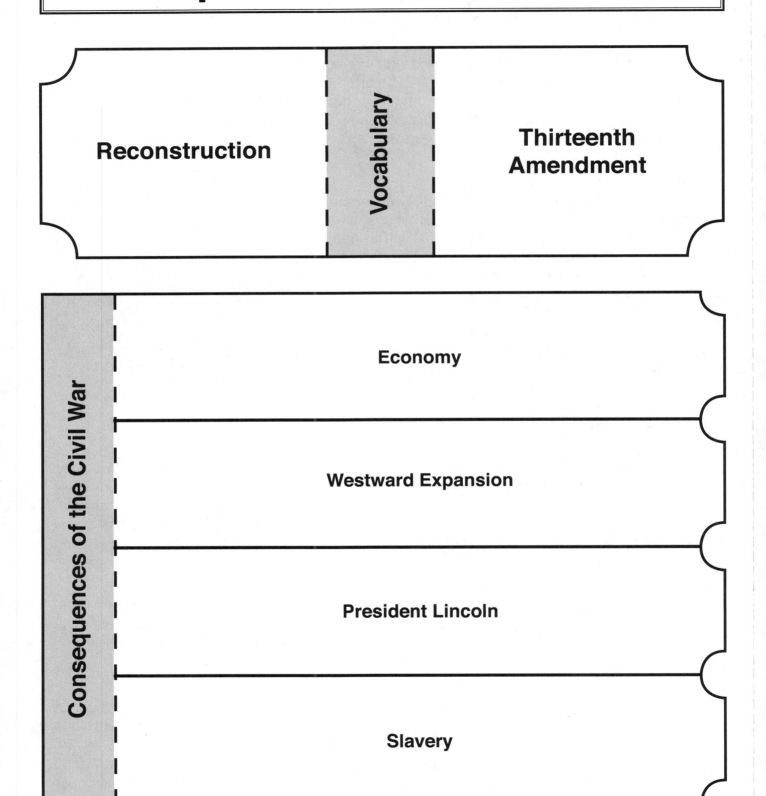

Reconstruction

Vocabulary

Thirteenth Amendment

Consequences of the Civil War

Economy

Westward Expansion

President Lincoln

Slavery